Old Jack

Stonewall Jackson House
Lexington, VA
2006
Maud Kashner

Old Jack

Life of Stonewall Jackson

by Marta Kastner
Illustrations by Carole Roberts

Cedar Hill Press
2005

This book is dedicated to the visitors of the Stonewall Jackson House in Lexington, Virginia, and to all others who want to hear about the man behind the legend, the private Thomas J. Jackson.

Cedar Hill Press
1093 Forge Road
Lexington, Virginia

© 1993 by Marta Kastner
All rights reserved

Library of Congress
Catalog Card number 93-091388

ISBN   0-9637343-0-x

Printed by The News-Gazette Print Shop
109 South Jefferson Street
Lexington, Virginia 24450

First Printing   1993
Second Printing 1996
Third Printing   2000
Fourth Printing 2005

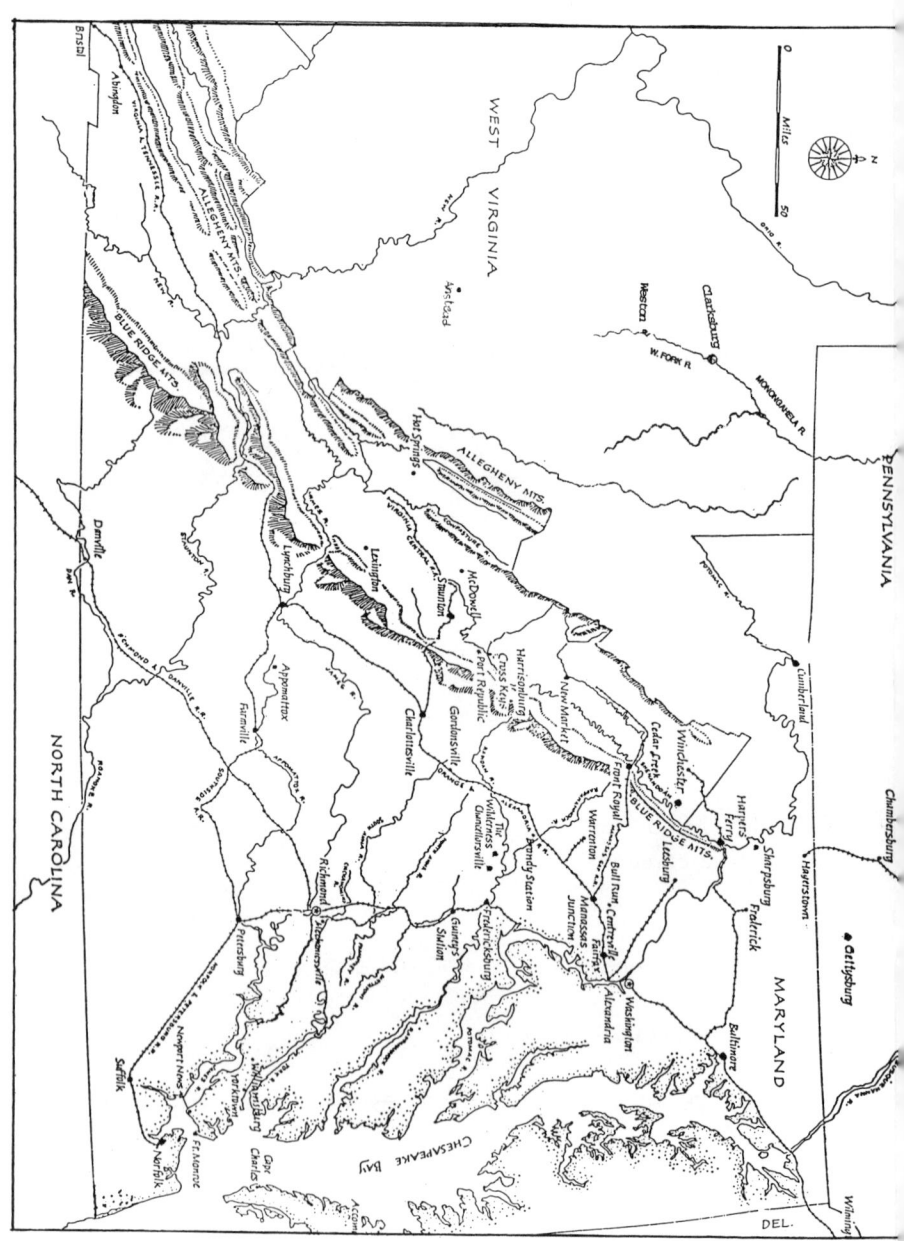

CONTENTS

Old Jack - Preface i
I. Roots and Family 1
II. A Most Independent Lad 4
III. Jackson at West Point 11
IV. You May Be Whatever You Resolve To Be 16
V. The Mexican War 21
VI. A Soldier in Peacetime 29
VII. A Mistaken Sense of Duty 36
VIII. Lexington and VMI 40
IX. Home Life in Lexington 46
X. Second Marriage 54
XI. To Arms 68
XII. Family Life in War 74
XIII. Stonewall Jackson's Way 82
XIV. Jackson and Fame 94
XV. His Time Had Come 102
XVI. Return to Lexington 108
War Casualties 111
Epilogue 112
Chronology of Jackson's Life 114
People and Events 117
Notes 135
Bibliography 155
Index 157

OLD JACK

They called him "Old Jack," sometimes fondly, at other times with exasperation. The full name was Thomas Jonathan Jackson. Even more people knew him as General Stonewall Jackson.

"Old Jack" was bestowed on him when he was a youngster because he always seemed older than his years, and it followed him for the rest of his days. At the West Point Military Academy lack of social graces made fellow cadet Dabney Maury say: "In my opinion Cadet Jackson of Virginia is a jackass."[1] Later his students at Virginia Military Institute called him "Tom Fool" or worse, and his troops had any number of other names for him such as "Old Blue Light"[2] for his piousness and "Fool Tom Jackson" for stubbornness.

He was known for his earnestness, not for his wit. He always followed his inner vision and did not worry how he appeared to others, but this characteristic also made him a source of amusement to many. Maggie Preston, who loved him dearly, said: "He was voted eccentric in our little circle because he did not walk in the same conventional grooves as other men," and, "Everyone who met him felt that they had never known just such another man."[3]

This short book brings together true stories and tall tales which were told about him when he was still alive and remembered after his untimely death in May 1863. These stories are not about the military man or the Civil War hero - that I leave to the military historians - they show instead the human, ordinary face of this extraordinary man.

In the course of research I have not unearthed any new materials, most every aspect of Jackson's life has been covered, probably much better, by other writers, but I have used whenever possible original sources. Some interesting but peripheral information has been relegated to the Notes section. I have also added a short chronology of Jackson's life and a section on Who Was Who around him.

I.
ROOTS AND FAMILY

Jackson was born in 1824 in Clarksburg, (now West) Virginia as the third child of Jonathan and Julia Neale Jackson. January 21st is celebrated as his birthday, but it may not be correct. Tom himself was in doubt about his birth date, so in his teens he asked the family physician, Dr. James McCally, who told him he was born shortly before midnight on January 20th, and not early morning on the 21st.[1]

His childhood was sometimes difficult. When he was two years old Tom lost his father and an older sister to typhoid fever and gained a baby sister. This all happened in a period of three weeks.[2] His father had been a lawyer and came from a good family, but he left little property and many debts. Some people said that these were mainly gambling debts, others said that Jonathan Jackson was a friendly fellow who freely co-signed his friends' promissory notes.

Jackson's mother tried to hold the family together by sewing and teaching school and later by remarrying to another impecunious lawyer, Blake B. Woodson. But still she could not keep the children. They had to be farmed out to various relatives. Julia Jackson Woodson died in Ansted in 1831 when Tom was just seven years old. As an adult, Tom wanted to put a stone on her grave, but he could not find it.

There is still some confusion about where Tom spent his early years. The reports of various family members differ. He probably lived with his mother until he was about five years old, and then he and his younger sister Laura were sent to his step-grandmother Jackson at the Jackson Mill, while Tom's older brother Warren was sent to maternal relatives, the Neales.

Jackson Mill was the family seat, so to speak, a sturdy two story log structure located near Weston in Lewis County, Virginia. A number of relatives were living there, aunts, uncles, cousins; and Tom just blended in. He seemed to have been happy there. When his grandmother Jackson died and the rest of the family scattered, Tom was left in the Jackson Mill with his uncle Cummins E. Jackson.[3]

Uncle Cummins was a character. He was a large man, more than 6 feet tall and some 250 lbs, gregarious but opinionated. He had many friends and probably as many enemies whom he was in the habit of suing. Cummins was fond of his young nephew, and Tom returned his affection. But there were some who thought Cummins' influence on Tom was bad, since he was a bachelor, liked to take a drink, and was not a church goer. Stories about Cummins mention both his strength and his drinking; he could carry a sack of flour under each of his arms, and there was one time when on a bet he hoisted a barrel of hard cider and drank from the bung hole.[4]

ROOTS AND FAMILY

Shortly after Grandmother Jackson died, when Tom was about twelve years old, the family decided to get him away from Cummins and sent him to Harrison County to live with another relative, his uncle Isaac Brake. This was not a success. In a short time young Tom ran away from his uncle Brake, and appeared wet, tired and hungry at another relative's house in Clarksburg. He explained it with a typically laconic Jacksonian remark, "Uncle Brake and I don't agree. I have quit him." Nothing would make him go back. He was allowed to return to Cummins and the Jackson Mill, where he lived until his eighteenth year.

Uncle Cummins liked horses, and he put Tom on a horse when the boy was seven years old. Cummins was also a horse racing man. There was a small race track near the Jackson Mill where Tom, once he reached his teens, rode for him as his jockey. In later years much derision was heaped on Jackson's horsemanship, his seat in the saddle was seen as ungainly, he had his stirrups awkwardly high, and he looked as if he was about to fall off his horse. Compared to the dashing riders at West Point or fellow officers such as Jeb Stuart, Robert E. Lee, or Turner Ashby, Jackson was not impressive. And yet, he must have been better than his reputation indicated. During the Civil War he could stay in the saddle for a day and a half, and ride fifty miles at a stretch even while dozing off. And as uncle Cummins' jockey he rode to victory in a number of races. Once, in a very special race Cummins would not let Tom ride his favorite horse, Kit, but instead rode him himself and lost to the chagrin of his friends who all had a lot of money wagered on the race. Many of these friends thought that this would not have happened had Tom been the rider.[5]

Uncle Cummins caught Gold Rush fever and in early 1849 went to California where he died from typhoid in December of the same year. He was forty-six years old. Tom was, at that time back from the Mexican War, stationed at Fort Hamilton in New York. When he heard the news, he wrote to his sister: "This goes to my heart. Uncle was father to me."[6]

II.
A MOST INDEPENDENT LAD

Tom kept his own counsel from the time he was a boy. To earn spending money he used to fish in the nearby West Fork of the Monongahela River and sold his catch to the local gunsmith Conrad Kester. One day as he was coming home with a large pike another neighbor, Colonel John Talbott, stopped him and offered one dollar for it. Tom said no, he would not sell it. So Talbott raised his offer to $1.25. To his great surprise this generous offer was again refused. When he asked why, Tom offered this explanation : "Colonel Talbott, I have an agreement with Mr. Kester to sell him for 50 cents any fish over a certain size. Mr. Kester has taken some fish which were smaller, so he is going to get this big fish for 50 cents."[1]

Some time later his older brother Warren, who had been living with other relatives in Ohio, appeared at the Jackson Mill. Warren had a wonderful idea, a money-making scheme. He wanted Tom to come with him to the Mississippi River where they were going to build a raft, float to some island on the river and settle there. There they would get rich by cutting wood and selling it to steamboats going down the river.[2] This was in 1836 when Warren was sixteen years old and Tom was twelve.

First the boys went to Ohio where a relative owned James Island on the Ohio River. On their way, they had to cross some 80 miles of mostly wild country. From there they headed down the river to Belleville to other relatives, and then south to the Mississippi where, somewhere in the southwestern corner of Kentucky, they found their island.

On this island the boys lived in a patched up shack. Other than malaria, which they both caught, they enjoyed their independent life and stayed there for several months. They did not get rich, but they made some money with which each boy bought a small leather trunk. Tom gave his to sister Laura and she took good care of it.[3] It can be seen today in the Jackson House, Lexington, Va.

Tom's education was spotty. A friend of his later wrote: "He was thought by his uncle Cummins to be the dullest of the three children and in consequence received less education than Warren or Laura."[4] He attended classes of itinerant teachers who set up school in the neighborhood, but this was a few weeks here and a few months there, so he may have had less than a couple of years of schooling. When his brother Warren became a schoolmaster, Tom was impressed.

But he learned to read young, and as a boy he owned one book, the Bible. His best friend Joe Lightburn owned a book about the patriots of the American Revolution, "The Life of Francis Marion," by Mason (Parson) Weems. The boys used to go to the river bank and read each other's books and discuss their reading.[5] Lightburn also became a general during the Civil War, but he fought on the the Union side. After the war he became a Baptist minister. There is no record that Tom and Joe ever met on the battlefield.

Despite his limited schooling, Tom followed in his brother Warren's footsteps and became a school teacher. In the winter of 1840-41, he was hired to teach reading and spelling to three girls and two boys, all about eleven or twelve years old. The term lasted four months for which he was paid $5.64. He was at that time sixteen years old.[6]

His school was in a log cabin, not far from Jackson's Mill. It was supported by the Virginia "Literary Fund" which helped families without money to send their children to private schools, since there were no public schools then in the region. A model for penmanship, supposedly written by Tom for his pupils, exhorted them: "A man of words and not of deeds is like a garden full of weeds."[7]

We do not know whether or not Tom enjoyed teaching, but after several months, through the help of his uncle Cummins and a family friend, Col. Withers, he was offered a better job. On June 8, 1841, Thomas Jackson was appointed constable of Lewis County, (now West) Virginia. This was not an easy job for a skinny 17 year old boy. He was expected to collect bad debts, but the only authority he had was the law, which was not always honored, and his own ingenuity.

One time a widow asked him to collect a bad debt for her from a local man. But despite Tom's several attempts to collect it the man would not pay up. Tom was almost at his wit's end when he remembered that he had the right to seize the man's horse if he wasn't in the saddle and sell it to satisfy the debt. So he staked out the stable where this man usually stopped. When the man arrived and dismounted, Jackson leaped out from hiding and tried to grab the reins. He was not fast enough. The man jumped right back into the saddle and would not move. Jackson noticed that the stable door was low, allowing a horse to get through, but not with a rider. So although the man was hitting him with his whip Tom grabbed the reins and started to lead the horse into the stable. After some pulling he succeeded. The man had to jump off, Tom had the horse, and the widow received her money.[8]

Being a constable was not a bad job for a young man in Tom's position, but he wanted more. He was ambitious, he wanted to get rich, and he thought that education could help him. But he was a penniless orphan and college cost money. His only chance was to get an appointment to a school like West Point where the tuition was paid by the government.[9]

In 1842, when Tom was eighteen years old, such an opportunity presented itself. The local congressman, Samuel Hays, had that year an appointment to make to West Point, and Tom Jackson along with three other local boys applied. One of them was eliminated as being too young, but the three remaining lads had to take a test before a decision could be made. One of the young men, whose name was Gibson Butcher, did very well in mathematics, and so the appointment went to him. He too was an orphan from a prominent local family. Some said that Butcher's math score perhaps wasn't all that superior but that his friendship with the examiner's daughter tipped the scales.[10]

As it happened, Gibson Butcher arrived at West Point, took in the buildings, which looked to him like a jail, and the discipline felt like it too. After a few days he decided that education was not worth it - he was going home. This he did without telling anyone. On his way Gibson stopped at the Jackson Mill, where he told his friend Tom Jackson, "That is no place for me, you can have it," and left with him his letter of resignation.[11]

At this point, Uncle Cummins showed his mettle. He and Tom approached every important resident of the county for a letter of recommendation. Some people had doubts about Tom's qualifications, but he persuaded them, saying: "I know I am very ignorant. But I can make it up in study. I know I have the energy, and I think I have the intellect."[12]

Within a week they had a stack of letters and petitions, and before nine days were over, Tom was on his way to Washington to see Congressman Hays. He set out on horseback to catch the stage in Clarksburg which was to take him to the train. Uncle Cummins sent a young black boy with Tom to bring the horse back. However, Tom missed the stage. Rather than return home and wait for the next one, the two boys chased it for the next 20 miles before they caught up with it.[13]

When Tom arrived in Washington, Congressman Hays was surprised. He had no idea that Butcher had left West Point, and he was not pleased to get the news. It reflected on his judgment. He had recommended young Butcher to the Secretary of War, John C. Spencer, and now he had to advise the Secretary of the new developments. So when Tom Jackson came out with his stack of letters urging his own appointment instead, Congressman Hays was mollified. He wrote a letter for the Secretary of War praising Jackson's high moral character, cautiously mentioning his "improvable mind."[14] This no doubt due to Jackson's less than perfect academic credentials. However, Secretary Spencer seemed favorably impressed by Jackson's eagerness and enterprise, and immediately, on June 12, 1842, issued Tom a provisional warrant of appointment. Although Congressman Hays asked Tom to stay a few days in Washington to see the sights, the young man with his mind set on West Point refused the offer and continued on his way north.

There is a tale told about the impression Jackson made on Secretary Spencer, which may or may not be true. Apparently the Secretary, noticing Tom's name as well as his homespun clothes and his self assurance, told him : "Young man, you have a good name. If anybody at West Point insults you, give them a good beating and charge it to me."[15]

Yes, Jackson had a good name, his family was a fine one.

A MOST INDEPENDENT LAD

Tom's great-grandfather John Jackson came to America in 1748 and settled first in Maryland and later in Clarksburg, Virginia. He and his sons all fought in the Revolutionary War. Later generations included congressmen, judges and lawyers. Tom's father was sent to good schools and was admitted to the bar at twenty, supposedly through family influence, but there were early signs of trouble. After he was appointed collector of internal revenue, his accounts were found short by $3,500 and a relative, Congressman John G. Jackson, had to cover it. According to contemporary sources, Jonathan Jackson went through his inheritance dying in debt.[16]

Throughout his life Jackson seemed ambivalent about his father. He hardly ever mentioned his name. There were hints that he held a grudge against him. What was the basis for that was never spelled out. It could not have been merely that he left Tom an orphan at two years of age, or even that his death left the family in relative poverty. In those days this was common enough. The general assumption is that Tom knew about his father's reputation, and blamed him for the debts which so burdened his mother. And that he thought this could have been avoided if his father had spent more time lawyering and less carousing and gambling.

Some evidence comes from Tom's own mouth, or rather his pen. While in Mexico, Tom had a letter from sister Laura saying she was ill and concluding, "I may not live to receive your answer." Tom immediately tried to calm her fears, but then he added, "If your disease is incurable, then He may....receive you in His heavenly abode,... where I should hope to meet with you ....there with mother, a brother, a sister and yourself, and I hope a father...",- clearly Tom was not certain of his father's final destination.[17]

There may be a connection between Tom's feelings about his father and his middle name. When Jackson was born, and for the next eighteen years, he was known to one and all as Thomas

Jackson - no middle name. A middle initial "J." appeared for the first time in 1841, when he signed a pay receipt for teaching.[18] This was expanded into a full "Jonathan" (which was the name of his father) during his campaign to get into West Point, and afterwards it became a permanent part of his name. No explanation was ever offered why then, why at all. Some of his biographers touched on this point, and speculated whether this meant that in his teens Tom had come to terms with his late father and was willing to identify with him.

Tom did not have any difficulty in having his middle name accepted officially, at West Point or by other authorities, but it was different with his family. They insisted on just plain Thomas Jackson. As late as his third year at West Point, Tom was writing plaintively to his sister Laura to please address her letters to him as Thomas Jonathan Jackson because he was having difficulties getting them from the post office as there was another Jackson, Thomas K., in the school.[19]

III.
JACKSON AT WEST POINT

No matter how self-assured Tom Jackson was in planning his campaign to get to West Point, once he arrived there he found himself on the defensive. Suddenly he had to compete against young men from wealthy families, who had traveled, who had been privately educated, some of whom had several years of college. This was an entirely different game.

His arrival at the school did not pass unnoticed. He arrived later than the other cadets so he stood out. When he checked in he was dressed in his best gray homespun clothes, which fit him no doubt poorly, his big feet shod in dusty boots, and on his head he wore a large, coarse felt hat. His other possessions he carried in two weather-stained saddle bags.[1] He looked like what he was: a country boy, fresh from the mountains of Virginia. It was the wrong part of Virginia, poor, a bit uncouth, not at all like the Tidewater area on the other side of the mountains with its culture and gracious plantation life.

Appearances were noticed and taken seriously at the Point. After all, the cadets went there to become both officers and gentlemen. The three cadets who saw Tom arriving were watching him critically. What they saw was a slight young man with monstrously huge feet, walking head bent forward and looking straight ahead as if into space. He looked awkward, he looked ridiculous. But something of Jackson's determination to make good must have been apparent; Birkett Fry, Powell Hill and Dabney Maury checked him over and one of them remarked: "That fellow looks as if he has come to stay."[2]

Maury later went to meet Jackson, "To show interest in a fellow country-man in a strange land," but his lighthearted welcome was rebuffed. Dabney Maury was a plebe himself, but compared to Jackson he was a man of the world. He was twenty years old, son of a Navy captain, member of a distinguished family, and a graduate of the University of Virginia. When Maury introduced himself and offered help, Jackson responded, "In a manner so chilling," that Maury went away angry.[3]

Still, some weeks later Maury made another attempt to be friendly. This was during the cadets' summer encampment. Jackson was on duty policing the grounds while Maury and his friends were relaxing in their tent. When Maury jokingly told Tom to clean up all the cigar butts and trash around the camp, Jackson did not say anything, but with a look of cold fury, he marched away. Maury saw he had made a mistake. But he was a gentleman, so he told his companions: "I have made Cadet Jackson of Virginia angry and must at once humble myself and explain." He found Jackson in the guard tent where he told him: "Mr. Jackson, I find that I made a mistake in speaking to you in a playful manner - not justified by our short acquaintance. I regret that I did so." Jackson looked at him at length and coldly replied: "That is perfectly satisfactory, sir." It was then that Dabney Maury informed his friends: "In my opinion Cadet Jackson of Virginia is a jackass."[4]

But Tom's main problem was not social, it was his studies. One fellow cadet described it succinctly: "He had been to a common school, knew a little grammar, could add up a column of figures, but as to fractions, it is doubtful he ever heard of them."[5] As Jackson later told his cousin, Sylvanus White, he was given three weeks at the Point to learn the English grammar, which he did. He was expected to take algebra, geometry, chemistry, French, as well as drawing and other subjects, none of which he had before. Many of his fellow cadets found this not at all taxing after years of private tutoring, boarding schools and university studies. They were able to enjoy themselves, to socialize, while he had to spend all his time hitting the books.

The first year at the Point was a daily agony. Jackson was remembered as acutely suffering during his recitations and exams. When working at the blackboard solving math problems, he grimaced with the effort. He perspired so profusely that his classmates were sure he would flood the room,[6] and the chalk which he was clutching so hard would break, dusting his uniform white. In addition to his academic difficulties, he was also homesick. He managed to get through only by sheer force of will.

His greatest challenge came in the middle of his plebe (freshman) year, when the Academy passed on all the conditional appointments. This was in January, 1843. It was not just any recitation, but a formal military examining board conducted with much pomp and circumstance. Most of the cadets and faculty expected Cadet Jackson to fail. At the exam, he appeared grim and deadly serious. With a fierce concentration, mopping his sweaty face with his sleeve, he wrote on the blackboard. According to his friends, "His labored explanations fairly shouted his earnestness, and looks, chalk, sweat and moral virtue at war with mathematics left a lasting picture for the Academy's traditions."[7] Maury remembered that the examination, "pronounced a score or more 'deficient', leaving Jackson at the foot and McClellan at the head."[8] This was George B. McClellan from Philadelphia who came to West Point after two years at the University of Pennsylvania. The cadets who failed on the exam were dismissed from the Academy. Cadet Jackson just managed to squeeze through.

Such demands on top of his natural seriousness did not make him the best companion. Actually he didn't even try; he was not interested in social activities or eager to make friends. Intimidated by the enormity of what he had to learn, Jackson spent all his time studying, during the day as well as much of the night. At lights out, he would pile his grate with coals, and lying on the floor, study by this light as long as it lasted. Classmates used to say that he literally "burned" knowledge into his head.[9]

Tom was not a quick study, it was thought he had a slow mind, and even under the best of circumstances he had to work hard at his studies. One of his teachers later wrote about him: "He was not what is now termed brilliant, but he was one of those untiring matter-of-fact persons who never would give up an undertaking until he accomplished his object. He learned slowly, but what he got in his head he never forgot."[10] And Jackson's widow Anna remarked: "He was a diligent, plodding scholar, having a strong mind, though it was slow in development."[11] During the first two years at West Point, Jackson was constantly worried that he would fail and be sent back home.

His problems were compounded by his study habits. Instead of studying each day's current lesson, so that he could recite it in class the next day, he wanted to master the whole subject in depth. If he did not understand something he did not skip ahead but went back and kept working on it until he understood it perfectly, even if it meant not being up to date with his studies. His progress was slow and he lagged behind the class, sometimes by a few days, sometimes by weeks. The farther behind he got, the more anguished he was when he had to tell the instructor that he was unprepared for the day's lesson.[12] Even when eventually he caught up with the class, the old marks unfortunately counted against him in grading.

Jackson's least favorite subject was French, although drawing was a close second. In his first year in school, he ranked as seventieth in French in a class of eighty-three, which he improved in his second year to a rank of fifty-second. In drawing, he was sixty-eighth in second year and fifty-ninth in the third year. In math, he jumped from forty-fifth in his first year to a respectable eighteenth the next year. The subject where he excelled came in his last year. It was a course in ethics where he was fifth among sixty classmates. Other subjects also became easier and by the end of his fourth year, he graduated seventeenth in his class of fifty nine.[13]

As Jackson slowly got over the academic hurdles, he also acquired a few friends, although he never became hugely popular. He did not enjoy himself in a group but preferred the company of a single person with whom he could have serious conversations. Still, his principal recreation was long solitary walks in the countryside.

He was known in school as "the General", in honor of Andrew Jackson; not because they were related, (they were not, although they may have had a common ancestor because both families came from the same parish in Londonderry, Ireland,)[14] nor that his classmates were anticipating Tom's elevation to a flag rank, but the moniker was possibly a tribute to their shared homespun background. However, Tom's dogged determination to do the best he could was never disputed, and it won him respect. Fellow cadets were known to say that if they stayed one more year at the Point, the General would have ranked first in his class.[15]

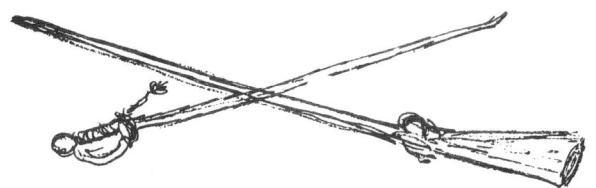

IV.
YOU MAY BE WHATEVER YOU RESOLVE TO BE

It was at West Point that Jackson started to compile a book of maxims which guided him for the rest of his life. This was common enough for young people of that time, but few of them took them as seriously and followed them as faithfully as Thomas Jonathan Jackson. He was an earnest young man, and he took life seriously. Among his maxims was not a single humorous one. "You may be whatever you resolve to be," was his favorite, and all his life he sincerely believed it. There were others:

Disregard public opinion when it interferes with your duty.
Say as little of yourself and friends as possible.
Speak but what may benefit others or yourself: avoid trifling conversation.
Resolve to perform what you ought; perform without fail what you resolve.
It is not desirable to have a large number of intimate friends, you may have many acquaintances, but few intimate friends.
Sacrifice your life rather than your word.[1]

In later years he had no time for journals, but he did not stop thinking about such things. In his reading, he underlined and annotated similar maxims so he would remember them. As an adult, he most often pondered religious matters, putting his total trust in God, following His word as far as he was able, and not worrying about events which were beyond his control. At other times, he had to be more down to earth. As a military commander, in 1862, he thought about military qualities and wrote: "Whilst I highly prize Military education - yet something more is required to make a general - judgment, nerve and force of character."[2]

There was also a hard, merciless side to Jackson. He showed it most often in a battle. When, during the Valley Campaign, one officer mentioned the bravery of the Union soldiers and said that he was almost sorry to see them fall, Jackson became indignant, "No, shoot them all," said Jackson, "I do not wish them to be brave."[3]

It is well known that Thomas Jackson, both before and after he became known as Stonewall, was a model of rectitude, and never boisterous or wild. That is never, but once. This happened during the heady July days of 1846, after his graduation from West Point. Tom and his fellow graduates had been commissioned as brevet rank second lieutenants and assigned to their army units, but first they were given a leave.

Tom was travelling home with several other fellow Virginians: Cadmus Wilcox, Archibald Blair Botts, Clarendon J. L. (Dominie) Wilson and Dabney Maury - who by this time had changed his opinion about Cadet Jackson of Virginia and who is responsible for the description of the following adventure.

The young officers, feeling their oats, arrived in Washington on a hot, humid day and checked into one room at the Brown's Hotel for the night. Cadmus Wilcox had been invited to dinner by the Secretary of War. Returning to the hotel after midnight and walking down the hall toward their room, he heard such noise that he couldn't imagine what was causing it. He heard raucous singing, loud beat of feet, and other rude sounds. The door was locked, so he knocked, but the response was more noise. Finally, according to Maury: "When at last admitted Cadmus found 'High Jinks' were enacted there. Poor Archie, in his fine new uniform, lay slumbering upon a bed, while Dominie and Old Jack, with only one garment, were singing with stunning effect Benny Havens Oh', and executing a barefoot backstep in time to the music. Each composed his own poetry in tones which resounded through the house and over the Avenue, till old Mr. Jesse Brown sent his compliments, with a request that they 'would stop that noise'." The song must have been a West Point's favorite which starts:

> Come, fill your glasses, fellows and stand up in a row,
> To singing sentimentally, we're going for to go;
> In the Army there's sobriety, promotion's very slow,
> So we'll sing our reminiscences of Benny Havens, oh!
> Oh! Benny Havens, oh! oh! Benny Havens, oh!

Maury added: "This was Old Jack's first and last frolic, to which in years long after his fame had filled the world he dimly alluded when he said he was too fond of liquor to trust himself."[4]

The high-minded maxims he wrote in his notebook did not help Tom in his relationship with the fair sex. Jackson had a problem with girls, and vice versa. He liked ladies and sought their company, but in their presence, he became even more shy and diffident than usual. He did fine with his sister Laura, but he was tongue tied with anyone else. Yet some girls liked him. It couldn't have been because he was amusing. Jackson just did not have the gift of gab; he had no small talk; he would speak only if he had something specific to say, so he usually remained silent.

What amused the girls was Tom's immense politeness and how he deferred to every female wish. They probably also appreciated his eager protection of feminine honor. When he was still living at the Jackson Mill, he once got into a fight with the town bully who had been pestering a local girl - Jackson won it too, even though the bully outweighed him.[5]

During Tom's only visit home from West Point in the summer of 1844, he was riding to church with a young lady, Miss Caroline Harris. Tom was dressed in his splendid new uniform, gray coatee with brass buttons and white pantaloons. As they were fording a shallow river Tom's horse stepped on a rock, stumbled and fell, dumping Tom into the stream. Without a word of complaint, Tom remounted his horse and rode on. At the Broad Run Baptist Church, he went inside in his dripping wet uniform, sat down next to Miss Harris, and stayed for the service.[6]

One wonders if his horsemanship had something to do with this mishap. Many people commented on how uncomfortable he looked in the saddle. Dabney Maury summarized the contemporary view on Jackson's horsemanship. "Old Jack was very clumsy in his horsemanship and with his sword, and we were painfully anxious as we watched him leaping the bar and cutting at heads. He would do it, but at the risk of his life." After explaining that Jackson had "a rough hand with the bridle, ungainly seat, and ....seemed in imminent danger of falling headlong from his horse,"[7] Maury concluded: "he could no more have become a horseman than he could have danced the german."[8]

Even in later years Jackson did not get high marks in gracefulness. Henry Kyd Douglas, who in every other respect worshipped Jackson, said: "In all his movements from riding his horse to handling a pen he was the most awkward man in the army," and, "Walking or riding the general was ungainly; his main object was to get over the ground."[9]

It seems that dancing was another area where Jackson did not shine. Dancing was taught at West Point, usually during the summer camps. This was no doubt to fulfil the second part in making the young men into officers and gentlemen. During these classes, the cadets danced with other cadets, and everyone was expected to take part. In winter, there may have been "hops" with young ladies, but it is unlikely that Jackson ever joined in them. He said in later years that during his four years at West Point he did not even speak to any young lady.[10]

In later years, his success with the Spanish senoritas in Mexico was often mentioned, but without any specifics. So we cannot be sure. The mores in Mexico were different, young ladies were closely chaperoned, and Jackson's special brand of formality, not to mention his middling fluency in Spanish, were most likely appreciated but did not lead to any intimacy. And perhaps his dancing improved.

V.
THE MEXICAN WAR

The Mexican war had just started when the West Point class of 1846 was graduating. Tom saw it as a wonderful opportunity. In peace, an army career was dull, tedious, and promotions were slow. But in a war, man could gain fame if he was lucky to find action.

To find action proved to be harder than he thought. Tom was assigned to the First Artillery under Captain Francis Taylor. They left New York August 19, 1846, and did not reach Camargo until October 31. But, there was no fighting in Camargo. Although it looked as though the war was winding down, they started for Monterey - which had been taken in a bloody battle by General Zachary Taylor only a month earlier. Tom acted as assistant commissary, in charge of guns, supplies, horses and such. Dabney Maury, who was with the mounted rifles, ran across Tom during that time and reported: "He worked at them (the guns) in the muddy roads as he used to do at West Point, and they had to move along."[1] It was a responsible job and Tom's battle to move the heavy guns was in a way heroic, but did not win him any kudos.

When they arrived in Monterey on November 29, they found it peaceful. Tom moved into a house on the outskirts of the town, where (he wrote to his sister Laura), there was a "beautiful orange orchard, and a fine bathing establishment with a pool twenty-five by thirty feet."[2] He was comfortable enough in Monterey but also frustrated, still pining for military glory. It was at this time, in winter 1846, that Tom met the man who in years to come would change the course of his life, not once but three times.

This man was Lieutenant Daniel Harvey Hill, from North Carolina, West Point class 1842. Hill was talking with another officer, Captain George Taylor, when an unusually serious and determined looking young man walked by. Captain Taylor remarked, "Do you know Lieutenant Jackson? No? ...He will make his mark in this war. I taught him at West Point. He never gave up on anything." Taylor continued, "He was not much of a student then, but if he had stayed at West Point another four years, he would have graduated at the head of his class."[3] Jackson was introduced, but did not contribute much to the conversation. It wasn't until a later walk on the beach with Hill that Jackson relaxed and became friendlier. Hill enjoyed his company; he was especially impressed when Jackson told him: "I really envy you men who have been in action. We who have just arrived look upon you as veterans. I should like to be in one battle."[4] As he was saying it, he was no longer shy, but his face lit up with such enthusiasm that Hill remembered this moment for years afterwards.

Eventually Jackson was given his wish. This happened after

THE MEXICAN WAR

his company joined General Winfield Scott and took part in the capture of Vera Cruz, some 350 miles south of Monterey. At first, the action seemed too successful. General Scott landed his troops on the shore with hardly a shot fired, which did not satisfy Tom's dreams of glory. The siege of the city was better, especially to an artillery man like Jackson. After three weeks, on May 29, 1847, Vera Cruz surrendered. General Scott's losses were nineteen men killed, sixty-three wounded.

As far as Tom was concerned, this was better but not yet enough. Feeling a little let down he wrote to his sister Laura : "I presume you think my name ought to appear in the papers, but only those who have independent command are as a general rule spoken of." He added to it that, "If an officer wishes to distinguish himself, he must remain long in service until he obtains rank; when he receives praise not only for his efforts, but for the efforts of the officers and men under him."[5]

Jackson's letters to Laura were full of military analysis, and one wonders if the young woman, who had been recently married, was really interested in it all. If she wanted to share it with friends, she had to be careful. Some things, such as Tom's criticism of General Scott and the description of the General as "the most vain and conceited," which he wrote to his uncle Isaac Brake, were perhaps a bit presumptuous, as Tom was well aware, so he admonished them: "You will take particular care, that neither this nor any subsequent letter gets into a newspaper."[6]

After Vera Cruz, Tom was promoted to a full Second Lieutenant which was good news . The bad news was that he had to stay behind in Jalapa on garrison duty, while others were off to Mexico City. Tom was deeply disappointed. To Laura he wrote, "It may have been His (God's) means of diminishing my excessive ambition, and after having accomplished His purpose, whatever it may be, He then in his infinite wisdom may gratify my heart."[7] But he found Jalapa a pretty town and otherwise enjoyed his life there.

In early May he also wrote her about studying Spanish and about the ladies of the town, "I am in fine quarters and making rapid progress in the Spanish language and have an idea of making some lady acquaintances shortly."[8] In another letter, he again mentioned, "There are many pretty ladies here, but you must not infer from this that you will have one of them for your sister-in-law, for such is not my intention at present and not theirs I hope."[9] One can safely assume that the 'pretty ladies' motivated him to learn Spanish - and learn it fast.

Charming as the Mexican ladies were, they could not hold Jackson's attention forever. After seven months on garrison duty, an opportunity presented itself to join the Company of Captain John Bankhead Magruder. "I wanted to be near the enemy in the fight; and when I heard that John Magruder got his company I bent all my energies to be with him, for I knew if any fighting was to be done, Magruder was 'on hand'."[10]

That was the plus side for Jackson, the minus side was Magruder's personality. Not many wanted to serve under him. The Virginia born Magruder was known far and wide as "Prince John" for his flamboyant almost imperial social style, but he was also a strict disciplinarian, ill tempered and hard to please. In many aspects, he was just the opposite of Lieutenant Jackson. But Magruder was hot, he always went to the center of the action. Jackson figured that the price was right. As it turned out, he and Magruder complemented each other and got along fine.

In early August 1847, Jackson was on his way to attack Mexico City. Mexico City was the headquarters of the Mexican general Santa Anna and everyone expected it to be heavily defended. They were right.

In an early skirmish, the enemy had much bigger guns, but Lieutenant Jackson acquitted himself well enough to earn a promotion to brevet captain. He had to take over command for a wounded officer and later Magruder reported: "Lt. Jackson advanced in handsome style, and being assigned by me to the post so gallantly filled by Lt. Johnstone, kept up the fire with briskness and effect."[11] That was on August 19th, 1847.

Jackson's moment of glory came on Monday, September 13, 1847, at Chapultepec, when the Americans got caught in a heavy barrage of enemy fire. They had not been able to reconnoiter the terrain, and Jackson and his guns were far in the front, in fact so far in front they were practically cut off from the rest of the troops. In the heavy shelling, his men panicked and abandoned their guns. At this point, Jackson strode forward, and while walking on the road in full view of the enemy, he shouted: "See, there's no danger! I am not hit!"[12] This gave the men heart and slowly, at first one sergeant then several men, then the rest, crawled out of the ditch where they had been hiding and began manning the guns.[13]

At about this time, a messenger came with an order to retreat. He was told by Jackson: "No! With fifty experienced men we can overrun the battery ahead!" Then Magruder rode out to him, and had his horse killed under him. Magruder too favored retreat, but after he looked over the situation he agreed with Jackson. While Jackson continued to press ahead, word went back from Magruder for support. This arrived, foremost among them Daniel Harvey Hill and Barnard E. Bee. Before long, the Chapultepec Citadel fell.[14] On September 14, Mexico City surrendered to the Americans.

This action earned Tom Jackson a promotion to brevet Major - at a price, however - this was the only time in his life when he told a barefaced lie. As he was strutting in front of his men, exhorting them to continue fighting, one enemy shot went between his legs, and he was acutely aware of the danger.[15] Still he said what he had to say to continue the attack. He admitted to the lie in later years, in the days after the attack he just said, "The only anxiety I felt was that I might not meet enough danger to make my conduct conspicuous."[16] Jackson also said that under such circumstances, under fire, he was conscious of a more perfect command of all his faculties, and of their more clear and rapid action, than at any other time. It was exalting, he rejoiced in it.[17]

His gallant behavior also earned him a promotion. "For gallantry in the battle of Contreras and Cherubusco on the 20th of August," Jackson was breveted a captain, and for Chapultepec on September 13, he was breveted a major. "There were only five or six who received double brevets," wrote his widow in her memoirs; Jackson was the only one from his West Point class.[18]

The only other time Jackson felt in danger was also in Mexico, when he was given a chest of money to guard overnight. As he was sleeping, he suddenly found himself shaken and heaved out of his bed. He jumped up and searched his room but found nothing. So he lay down again, but the same thing happened again. That really frightened him. Finally he heard shouts. Running outside, he realized that it was an earthquake.[19]

Jackson's bravery and military cunning had been noticed by his superiors. As he proudly wrote to Laura, his name was mentioned in dispatches by Generals Pillow and Worth, and even by no lesser personage than the supreme commander of all the American forces in Mexico, General Winfield Scott.

In addition, General Scott singled him out, albeit in a rather heavy handed way. This happened at a levee given by the general shortly after the capture of Mexico City. During a receiving line, Lieutenant Thomas Jackson was presented to the general, who drew himself up, put his hands behind his back and in an exaggeratedly serious tone of voice said, "I don't know that I shall shake hands with Mr. Jackson," causing Tom to turn crimson in confusion. By that time, everyone in the room was listening as General Scott boomed on, "If you can forgive yourself for the way you have slaughtered those poor Mexicans with your guns, I am not sure that I can,"[20] after which the general shook hands firmly and at length with the young man.

The duties as an officer of an occupying army were light, but time did not weigh heavily on Jackson's hands. He kept himself busy by studying history and the Spanish language, which he learned by reading Lord Chesterfield's letters to his son both in English and Spanish,[21] because he could not find any Spanish grammar or textbook. He also began to show an interest in religion. He went at it with his characteristic thoroughness: he visited Mexican cathedrals, spent some time with monks in a monastery and through the introduction of friends sought advice and information from the Archbishop Irisarri of Mexico. After much deliberation, he concluded that Catholicism was not for him. What he was seeking was something simpler and more basic. But he did not seek it immediately; D.H. Hill later stated that, "In Mexico, he (Jackson) had no particular regard for religion."[22]

The local social scene offered other pleasures. Despite the fact that the Americans were occupying forces, they were warmly received by the Mexican society. Jackson continued with his Spanish and became reasonably fluent in it, which gave him an entree to some of the best families. In March 1848, he wrote to Laura, " I think that I pass my time more agreeably than the greater portion of the officers of the army."[23]

The nine months he spent in Mexico City were the most lighthearted of Jackson's life. He became a dandy. He had comfortable rooms in the national palace where he started the day with hot coffee or chocolate in bed. He bought a good horse. He went for rides on the Paseo, visited his Mexican friends, played cards, and attended Sunday balls where he danced with the local beauties.

This dandyish existence was perhaps out of character for him, but he enjoyed it. He wrote about it to Laura, who, living in rural Beverly, Virginia, did not approve of his spending money on clothes and pleasures. Tom tried to explain: "You speak of my fine horse as being in your opinion extravagant (he paid $180 for it), but if an officer wishes to appear best, he should appear well in everything. I bought the horse, having plenty of money and need for him, and have since been offered three hundred and fifty dollars for him."[24]

Jackson was paid $140 a month while he was with Magruder, but having been transferred again to Capt. Taylor, he was paid slightly less. Yet he wrote to Laura: "I have plenty of money, and I am in the long run economical. Here everything is dear. I dress as a gentleman should who wishes to be received as such. I do not gamble, nor spend my money, as I think, foolishly."[25]

Soon Jackson was able to converse in Spanish with the local senoritas, and he found them to his liking - one in particular. The name of the favored young woman has not been left to history, but Tom's friends suspected that he was in love. His nephew, Tom Arnold, speculated that she may have given him the inkstand adorned with doves[26] that he brought home as a souvenir. Writing to Laura on October 26, 1847, Tom slipped in an aside: "I think I probably shall stay many years here, and may possibly conclude (although I have not yet) to make my life more natural by sharing it with some amiable Senorita." Laura did not think much of the idea, and as it happened, Jackson left Mexico in June or July, 1848, still a bachelor.[27]

VI.
A SOLDIER IN PEACETIME

If Jackson found military life exciting in war, it was not true for peacetime. This was not surprising. Instead of battles, there was just the daily routine at Fort Hamilton, N.Y., enlivened by an occasional trip to other commands to sit on a court martial. Fortunately, Tom was back with the company of his first commander, Francis Taylor, who took interest in him and introduced him to what he called "personal religion". There was not much to do at Fort Hamilton, so discussing points of religious doctrine with one's commanding officer filled the time.

Tom attacked it with his characteristic fervor. He carefully studied the religious writings, and finally, on Sunday, April 29, 1849, he was baptized in the Episcopal church. Taylor was one of his sponsors. However, Jackson was careful to stipulate his terms: he wanted to be sure this did not oblige him to become an Episcopalian.[1] He suspected that he had not been baptized as a child; all he wanted at this time was to join the Christian community.

Jackson remained tolerant about Christian denominations for the rest of his life. During the Civil War, he attended other than Presbyterian services and arranged to have Roman Catholic masses for those who wanted them. One clergyman described Jackson's Sunday observances in camp, "So we had a Presbyterian sermon, introduced by Baptist services, under the direction of a Methodist chaplain, in an Episcopal church."[2]

Early in his stay at Fort Hamilton, Jackson asked for a leave and went to see his sister Laura Arnold in Beverly, (West) Virginia. During this visit, his nephew Tom Arnold got to know his uncle Tom and started to develop a life long admiration for him. In later years, Thomas Arnold collected letters Jackson wrote to the various members of the Arnold family and published them in a book along with other incidents from Jackson's life. The following story, showing the difficulties of travel in those days, comes to us from this book.

After his visit at the Arnolds in Beverly, Jackson planned to go to Washington to pay some courtesy visits at the Capitol. Jackson's leave was short, and he had a tight schedule. But there are two mountain ranges between Beverly and Washington, and in those days, there was little or no public transportation over them. So Jackson borrowed a horse from his brother-in-law, Mr. Arnold, to ride over to Virginia's Bath County, where in Hot Springs he could catch a stage. This took overnight. In the evening, he stopped at a farmer's house, asked for lodging and to please have his horse ready at 4 a.m., as he had to leave early. Not being much of a talker, that was about all Jackson said. The farmer, an elderly German, happened to recognize the horse, a large black beast, as belonging to Mr. Arnold, and he became convinced that his guest was stealing it. After all, why else was he so closemouthed and wanted to leave so early? So when 4 a.m. arrived, there was no horse ready, and furthermore, Jackson was given to understand he was not going to get his hands on the horse at all. Jackson had a stage to catch, he was determined, and he was angry, but not as determined as the old man. The two stubborn men got into a big argument. It was not until much too late that Jackson persuaded the farmer to let the horse go, so Jackson missed his stage and had to catch the next one two days later.[3]

It is hard to say when Jackson started worrying about his health. Some say that 'Tom's old complaint' or 'Tom's problem' may have appeared when he was just a boy, that he was a finicky eater, and he did not grow and gain weight as well as he should. "According to family accounts," wrote one of his biographers, "he suffered from the same trouble (dyspepsia) as a boy and was advised to take as much outdoor exercise as possible to combat it."[4] Starting with West Point and throughout his life, he worried about his digestion, circulation, his eyesight, hearing, rheumatism, chilblains, cold feet, liver, nervousness, neuralgia, tonsillitis (he had an operation for that), distortion of the spine and any number of other real or imagined symptoms of ill health. He became convinced that, "my afflictions were decreed by Heaven's Sovereign for my offenses."[5]

These spells of ill health seemed to come and go. When he was at West Point, Jackson always studied sitting bolt upright without touching the back of his chair because he believed it kept his organs in alignment. Tom thought it was beneficial, but his classmates found it weird. Fellow cadet, U.S. Grant, later described him, " He was a fanatic whose delusions took strange forms - hypochondria, fancies that an evil spirit had taken a possession of him."[6] In November 1845, his final year at West Point, he wrote Laura, "My constitution has received a severe shock,"[7] but did not go into specifics. In the same letter, he assured her that he was gradually recovering.

From Mexico, he frequently reported on his health, mostly

favorably. This was the healthiest period of his life. In one letter he wrote, "Cold in this climate is very different from what it is in ours. Here it can by care generally be cured in thirty-six hours. Consumption is almost unknown."[8]

It was also in Mexico where he learned to love fruit, for which he later in life became notorious. During the Civil War, after he became a general, he frequently sucked on half a lemon, because he said it helped his dyspepsia. With his battered cap pulled low over his eyes and the half lemon imbedded in the dark whiskers, he gave his orders. Lemons being scarce in the Confederate army, his men wondered where and how he obtained them. But they must have developed a certain affection for it, because after his death, a lemon, or half a lemon, has sometimes appeared on his grave in Lexington, as an affectionate token from his admirers.

His quest for fruit embarrassed him once during the Civil War. It was during a march when he happened to see a persimmon tree covered with fruit, which he declared was his favorite food. He went to the tree and climbed on a branch where he sat and ate until he was full. But then, to the great amusement of the passing troops, he was stuck and could not get down. His aide had to ask the men to make a skid for him from a picket fence to slide him down.[9]

When Jackson returned from Mexico, his health complaints increased dramatically. During his visit to his sister in the Virginia mountains, he caught rheumatism and suffered with it for several months. In a letter, he reported to her that he was under the care of "one of the first medical men of New York City", and that the doctor probably would not approve of him writing letters at all. Later, he complained of weak eyes ("I could not look long at objects through the window, ...I was reduced to the necessity of masking my looking glass, on account of its reflection,")[10] and still later, he again came down with dyspepsia as well as other illnesses. This all happened in a period of six months. He finally consulted a physician in New York City, Dr. Larry

Barney, who, after examining him, suggested that he should get married, "A man in the prime of life, considered rather handsome by the ladies, needs exercise best provided by the marriage bed," was the advice.[11] Jackson was then twenty-five years old.

Laura complained about her eyes too, so Tom deluged her with advice. "Remember that the best physicians are opposed to straining that important organ; spectacles should be the last resort, I would advise you not to use them as long as you can do without them, at the same time avoiding pain."[12] Another time he recommended that she take a basin of warm water and place her face into the water, opening and closing her eyes, "as long as she can hold her breath". He himself used to do it as often as six times daily.

Jackson suffered from eye problems all his life. When he lived in Lexington, he complained of spots floating in front of his eyes. Most of the time he refused to read or write with artificial light; sometimes even during the war, when dispatches came after dark they either would be read to him by his aides or they had to wait until the next day.

According to his old classmate, Dabney Maury, Jackson was convinced that one of his legs was larger than the other, as well as was one of his arms.[13] Many of those who knew him remarked that he often rode in the saddle with one arm held high above his head. He thought that his body was out of balance, and so the purpose of this was to drain the blood from the arm back into his body. There were people who wondered if perhaps this habit did not contribute to Jackson's wounding during the first battle of Manassas, where he was hit in the hand. Others swear that the lifting of the hand was a sign that Jackson was praying.

However, as in Mexico, Jackson was extremely healthy during the Civil War. He shed his usual illnesses, so that his friends and especially his wife remarked on his health and vigor. The only times when something bothered him was a spell of fever during the Seven Days battles and an ear ache in the winter at Moss Neck. Even the shot to his finger at the first battle of Manassas did not slow him down. Although the army surgeon wanted to amputate it, while he was turning around to get the instruments, Jackson walked out of the tent and rode away. He had the finger attended by another physician, Dr. McGuire, who put a splint on it and told Jackson to bathe it as much as possible in cold water. Jackson followed this prescription religiously for the next several weeks, pouring water on the hand many times a day, and indeed, in time, it not only healed, but he regained almost full use of the hand.[14]

For his other illnesses, Jackson treated himself mostly by a regime of exercise and diet. He took it enormously seriously and devoted much time to it. In one long and detailed letter to Laura, he explained, "I have strictly adhered to my wholesome diet of stale bread and plainly dressed meat (having nothing on it but salt)," and continued at great length about what foods to eat and when, and what to avoid, urging her to follow it as well.[15] He himself refused to use pepper on his food because he believed it made his left leg weak. He also urged Laura to take plenty of exercise "no less than three hours a day," for best results. We know that he was following his own advice. He wrote Laura that she and her husband might not find him a very pleasant house guest because his health regime occupied so much of his time and energy, "I am more particular in my rules than any person of your acquaintance."[16]

At Fort Hamilton, despite his many professed illnesses, Jackson enjoyed going into society, but he was a most unusual guest. He would not eat his hosts' food, he believed that rich food did not agree with him. He liked soft food, such as oatmeal and cereals. So he brought his own.

Jackson knew what was proper, but if in his own judgment he had a good reason to ignore it, he did. He did not worry what others thought about him. He brought his packages of cheese and crackers not only to informal gatherings, but also to the balls at Fort Lafayette and to the great formal receptions on Governor's Island, which were attended by all dignitaries in the area, and were known for their excellent food and drink.[17]

He also had firm ideas on going to bed early. No matter what the occasion, he went home shortly after taps. Once some young ladies at Fort Hamilton plotted to delay him. It happened at the home of James C. Church. The young Misses Church persuaded him to play cards and made it such an exciting and jolly occasion that they hoped he would forget about time. But no. Although Jackson seemed to be having a good time, as soon as he heard the taps, he rose, put down his cards, said farewells all around the room and left.[18] No wonder that the New York society considered him an eccentric.

VII.
A MISTAKEN SENSE OF DUTY

In autumn of 1850, Jackson was transferred to Fort Meade, Florida, some fifty miles east of Tampa. He reached it shortly before Christmas. Florida at that time was a frontier state with none of the graciousness of New York. Tampa had a population of two hundred, Fort Meade much less; most of the troops lived there in tents and suffered from heat and insects.

The Company had four officers, and Jackson was second in command under Captain (Brevet Major) William H. French, whom Jackson knew from Mexico. Their mission was to restore peace after the Seminole wars. In March, Jackson wrote his sister: "I have just returned from an eight days scout, in which I saw about twenty deer in one forenoon. I could find no Indians.

I traveled more than one hundred miles without seeing a house."[1] Other than surveying the country and the construction of the fort itself, there was little else to do.

At first, things went well enough. Jackson enjoyed the scouting trips even if he did not meet any Seminoles - there were only about three hundred of them left in the whole state. But he did not find his fellow officers congenial, least of all his commanding officer. In his letters to Laura, he hinted at the boredom and other problems but assured her that he did not want to give up his military career. "It is doubtful whether I shall relinquish the military profession, as I am very partial to it," he wrote her.[2] After two months at Fort Meade things started going downhill.

First, Jackson applied for transfer to another company, and also, alternately, for a leave of absence of nine months to travel abroad. That was in February 1851. While this was being processed, he got into a disagreement with Major French about his duties - Jackson felt that Major French was usurping some of his responsibilities. Perhaps there was friction between them because both officers held the same rank. French, who graduated from West Point eight years before Jackson, was higher ranking only because his promotion came before Jackson's. Letters and reports were sent to headquarters with the upshot that Jackson was told that his duties were to obey his commanding officer, period.

While this was happening, Jackson received an informal inquiry from the Virginia Military Institute if he would be interested in teaching there. This unexpected offer of a new career may have influenced what happened next. First, Jackson ended all social contacts with Major French, and they communicated only in the most formal and official manner. Shortly afterwards, Jackson summoned several soldiers and non-commissioned officers and questioned them at length about rumors that Major French had been seen in rather compromising circumstances with the family servant Julia. Jackson had heard some rumors about it, and it disturbed him deeply, so he decided to follow it up.

When the news of this drifted to Major French, he put Jackson under detention for conduct unbecoming an officer. Jackson sat in the brig for thirty-eight days, during which both officers kept sending charges and counter charges about each other to the headquarters. Jackson wrote to the Adjutant General in Tampa a letter stating: "On being informed that Major French was guilty of conduct unbecoming an officer and gentleman, I considered it my duty to investigate the subject, and in consequence he has placed me in arrest." The specifics of the conduct were that French had, "remained for a portion of several nights and days at his old quarters with his female servant......that he sat with her on the same bed .... that he was seen walking with her in the directions of the woods ... that he did so frequently appear alone in company with her as to cause common talk."[3] This was followed by more letters with other charges, by both sides, with Jackson listing at least twenty-two charges all dealing with other matters than the servant girl. Most of them seemed to be trivial matters about day to day operations, such as sending express messages, French giving oral rather than written orders, saying that building materials were all local when windows and hardware were furnished by the quartermaster, and similar details. French called the charges "malicious, made with malicious intent, infamous, scandalous and frivolous," and he called Jackson among other things a liar.[4]

Jackson at that time was suffering from an especially virulent spell of ill health. He complained that he could not use his eyes to write at all, so Major French allowed him to use one of the other officers as a secretary. On June 20, a verdict arrived from headquarters: neither officer's charges had merit, no investigation was necessary. Jackson should be released and both officers should return to their duties. In the meantime, Jackson's request for a nine months leave was granted, so he was free to leave Ft. Meade and accept the teaching position at Virginia Military Institute in Lexington.[5] He planned to resign from the Army as soon as the French affair was settled and his name cleared.

A MISTAKEN SENSE OF DUTY

In the meantime, French, whose career was at stake, appealed to the highest authority, General Scott, the General in Chief. General Scott reviewed the charges and sent back a letter expressing regret about the behavior of both officers; he censured Jackson on his "most mistaken sense of duty,"[6] but let the original judgment stand. This letter arrived on August 27, 1851, when Jackson was already teaching at the Virginia Military Institute.

It is hard not to speculate whether Jackson's decision to leave the army prompted his behavior toward Major French or whether it was a result of it. D.H. Hill mentioned something about it - years later - without any names: that an officer pleaded with Jackson not to press charges against an officer so that his innocent wife would not hear about her husband's unfaithfulness. Jackson was supposed to have shed tears and replied that, "The thought of inflicting pain upon her was agony to him, but his conscience compelled him to prosecute the case."[7] The consensus is that despite the circumstances it was Jackson's conscience that fueled the affair, and this led him to resign from the army.

It is interesting that Jackson's family and some of his biographers completely ignored this rather bizarre period at Fort Meade. R.L. Dabney in his seminal work on Jackson covers it with: "His abode at this port seems to have been as uneventful as it was short, for he rarely made any allusion to it."[8] Thomas Arnold made no mention of the French affair at all in his book. Mrs. Jackson in her memoirs hints at something, but covers it in a sentence and a half. She wrote, "Major Jackson was ordered to Fort Meade, near Tampa Bay, in Florida, where he remained about six months. The warm climate he found enervating and injurious to his health, but a delightful change soon came, removing him to the bracing air of the Valley of Virginia."[9]

VIII.
LEXINGTON AND V M I

In 1851, Virginia Military Institute was twelve years old and had 117 students. The Superintendent, Colonel F.H. Smith, taught mathematics. There were three other full professors and several instructors, but the school needed someone to teach natural and experimental philosophy, and infantry tactics. The requirements set by the Board of Visitors were for a Virginian or Southerner, and graduate of West Point.

A number of such men existed, but for one reason or other not one could come to Lexington. A frustrated Colonel Smith went for advice to his friend, one Major Daniel Harvey Hill (formerly of US Army in Mexico), who taught mathematics at Washington College, just a stone's throw from VMI in Lexington. He gave him a copy of the "Army Register" and told Hill, "Find me a man there." As Hill was paging through the Register, he saw the name Thomas Jonathan Jackson, and he remembered the earnest young officer he had met in Mexico.[1] He pointed at the name telling Smith, "Here is your man. He was born in Virginia, graduated from West Point and he is an outstanding officer."

It is a pity that Jackson did not turn out to be also an outstanding teacher. True, he had been out of school for some years and had forgotten much what he had studied there, but that wasn't the problem. He said: "I can always keep a day or two ahead of the class," and "What I willed to do, I can do,"[2] and he was partly right. Where he, or rather his students, ran into difficulties was that he thought that everyone should study the way he did.

To prepare for his lectures, Jackson learned them by heart. He could not ad lib or improvise, so he wrote out both text and questions and answers, memorized them and presented them in class. He did not use a textbook or any notes when he lectured. Problems started if students did not understand something. Jackson's remedy was to repeat the passage using exactly the same words, and even the same intonation - which, given the fact he was teaching analytical mechanics, optics, acoustics and astronomy, did not help a lot. Since in his mind he had formulated the material in the most precise and concise way, he did not see any need for additional explanations, but many of his students did. Lenoir Chambers in his book says: "Jackson used the hard-and-fast West Point method teaching style without flexibility or imagination. He 'heard' rather than taught the lessons of the text. He had no gift for elucidation, no talent for explanation, no capacity to approach the same goal by another route." Another of Jackson's biographers, the Reverend R.L. Dabney, who served under him during the Civil War, explained it, "He lacked the peculiar tact of an eminent teacher" and furthermore, "He was not gifted with manual dexterity...his experiments were not brilliant, and sometimes they resulted in ludicrous blunders."[3]

Jackson did not lecture this way because he was lazy. During his ten years of teaching, he spent several hours each day preparing himself for his lectures. When he was finished with his classes, he went home and studied his notes for at least two hours. In the evening, he liked to review them; but given the fact that he would not read with artificial light, he had a problem, he had to do it from memory. Sometimes he stood at his desk in his study, or paced back and forth, but after his marriage to Anna, he preferred to stay in the family parlor where he placed a chair facing a wall, and there he sat, "dumb as a sphinx" according to Anna, concentrating and mentally reviewing the material until he was sure he knew it perfectly. Often his wife was entertaining visitors there, but Jackson would be totally oblivious to his surroundings, sitting like a stone statue in the corner. After an hour or two, he would stand up and join the company.[4]

Some historians suggest that Jackson's practice in memorizing a great deal of material and then recalling it in detail was useful to him during the war. He was able to fix in his mind details of terrain, disposition of forces and any number of other factors. During battles, he did not have to refer to notes or maps.

Jackson knew he had a problem with speaking in public, but he was not willing to accept his limitations. His motto was : "You may be whatever you resolve to be." Still, when he was asked to lead the church congregation in a prayer, he was so tongue tied that he could not say a complete sentence. His long pauses and mangled words made the prayer incomprehensible and embarrassed the congregation. The minister did not want to call on Jackson again, but he begged him to do it. "I must persevere in it," he said, "until I learn to do it aright."[5]

To help him with public speaking, Jackson decided to join a debating club. Lexington had one, a highly regarded literary and debating group called the Franklin Society, which met every Saturday evening. In 1853 Jackson became a member. His first efforts at public speaking were so unbelievably painful that no one thought he would keep up with it. Jackson grimaced, stumbled, repeated words, hesitated, floundered this way and that, making little or no sense and finally sat down.[6] Everyone was intensely uncomfortable, but not the speaker. He promptly fell asleep in his seat. His performance did not worry him at all, he felt that he had tried, had done his best, and that was the important thing. He was willing to try again, and eventually he got better.[7]

During the following seven years as a member of the Franklin Society, Jackson debated a number of topics sufficiently well to be at times on the winning end. No doubt the topic mattered as well as the presentation, but still he should get some credit. Jackson lost when speaking for prohibition, but he almost won on the need for women to have access to higher education. The vote on this was 8 for and 10 against. When debating if all human species were descended from a common origin, Jackson was on the affirmative side which won 8 to 1.

The people in Lexington did not know what to make of Jackson, but his habits amused them. His students called him "Tom Fool" and made him the butt of their jokes. They had plenty of reasons for that. Such as one hot day when everyone put on summer uniform, but Jackson appeared in class in his heavy winter woolens. When he was asked about it, he replied: "I have not received an order to change into summer uniform."[8]

Or when Colonel Smith had called him on a winter afternoon to his office and then had to step out, so he asked Jackson to wait for him. Unfortunately, he became distracted and forgot about Jackson and went home. Next morning when Colonel Smith returned to the office, Jackson was still sitting, bolt upright, in the chair. He was told to wait, he said, so he waited. Jackson spent the whole night there.[9] Jackson never disobeyed an order - and anything his commanding officer said to him, he took for an order.

There was also the case of the dropped brick. Apparently someone dropped a brick from a window as Major Jackson was walking under it. It missed him by just a few inches. Jackson did not even pause or look up, but continued on his way as if nothing had happened.[10] Just like at West Point, the cadets joked about his large feet. Often the blackboard in his section room was decorated with a drawing of huge feet, in a tribute to their size, and the cadets bestowed yet another nickname on him: "Square Box."[11]

A young man in Lexington once described him, "Old Jack is a character. He is as systematic as a multiplication table and full of things military as an arsenal."[12] His students did not appreciate it. He was notoriously clumsy with his scientific demonstrations and created more havoc than enlightenment. One of them wrote, "Optics . . . so very difficult and taught by such hell of a fool, whose name is Jackson."[13] Another of his students better at writing poetry than at science wrote:

> The V.M.I., Oh, what a spot,
> In winter cold, in summer hot,
> Great Lord Almighty, what wonder
> Major Jackson, hell and thunder![14]

Jackson was not a good disciplinarian. One of Jackson's biographers quotes Dabney Maury as saying that "..it was the custom of Jackson's students to create wanton disrespect in his section-room."[15] His students were usually loud and rowdy, while he paid no attention to it. Maury mentions that, "While Jackson was intently watching a student recite the lesson others would be bombarding each other with 'paper pellets'," (i.e. spitballs.) "He was imperturbable through it all."[16]

But when a cadet confronted him directly, he had to respond. On a couple of occasions, this resulted in a court martial. In one case, the cadet later challenged Jackson to a duel. Jackson refused to fight, but also refused to protect himself from an attack. A story has it that Jackson received a warning as to where the cadet was waiting for him and was told not to go there. "Let the assassin murder me if he will," he was supposed to have said, as he continued in his walk. When he came to the young man, he looked at him firmly, at which point the cadet turned away.[17] The cadet's name was James A. Walker, and although this resulted in his dismissal from VMI, he fought under Jackson during the Civil War, and became the last commanding general of the Stonewall Brigade. Thirty-nine years after the incident he acted as chief marshall at the unveiling of the Jackson monument in Lexington.

IX.
HOME LIFE IN LEXINGTON

Jackson liked Lexington. It was then, as now, a charming small town nestled in the Shenandoah Valley, graced by the Allegheny Mountains on the west and the Blue Ridge on the east. Shortly after his arrival, Jackson wrote his sister: "Of all the places that have come under my observation in the United States, this little village is the most beautiful. I am enjoying myself more than I have done in years."[1]

Lexington in the 1850s was a friendly town with about 1,200 residents. It called itself 'the Athens of the Valley' because in addition to the two colleges, VMI and Washington College (now Washington and Lee University), it was also a home to the private law school of Judge John W. Brockenbrough, and it had two other private schools, the Classical School for boys and girls and the Ann Smith Academy for girls, two weekly newspapers, not to mention two thriving bookstores. (Among the books which were sold there then was Uncle Tom's Cabin.) The town had many cultural activities and a lively social life.

Major and Mrs. Hill introduced Major Jackson to the local society, but, although Jackson tried, he did not quite fit in. He was reserved, courteous but stiffly formal. When he spoke, he expressed himself so precisely as if he were giving a deposition in a court of law. Young ladies could not engage him in banter, he would stand in front of them at parade rest, take their every remark literally and answer in monosyllables. In a relaxed society he "punctiliously performed courtesies due from young gentleman,"[2] and he was a fanatic about punctuality. Even his second wife, Mary Anna Jackson admitted that when she first met him she and her sisters used to make fun of him, "In social life Major Jackson was not what is called a 'society man,' indeed the very phrase seems an incongruity as applied to him," she wrote in her memoirs.[3]

One Washington College student described him: "He sat perfectly erect, his back touching the back of his chair nowhere, the large hands spread out, one on each knee, while the large feet sticking out at an exact right angle to the leg." And he did not say much. Another friend later commented: "If silence is golden, Old Jack is a bonanza."[4]

This habit of sitting rigidly upright, never lounging or even crossing his legs, became even more hilarious when the town people heard its reason: "He did it to keep his alimentary canal straight."[5] Just a mention of this could bring the local ladies into wild laughter.

Jackson was equally rigid in his passion for absolute truth. Once he got out of his bed late in the evening, dressed, and walked to the Institute to tell a student that he was mistaken when he marked the student's answer wrong. Another time Jackson walked in the rain to a house of a man because he mentioned to him that he had a casual conversation with a cadet in the barracks on Monday, when actually it was on the parade ground on Tuesday.[6] But his principle was "Find what is the right thing to do and then do it."[7] So he followed it. Another Lexingtonian remembers a conversation where someone said to Jackson: "As you remember, Lord Burleigh was Queen Elizabeth's great counselor," and Jackson responded, "I don't remember, I never knew it." A friend chided him that he was splitting hairs, but he did not think so. He said that he did not want to give an impression he knew something when he did not.[8] He said: "I have no gift for seeming."[9]

Jackson's close friends, and he had some, did not find him dull or eccentric. In a small group he enjoyed talking about things which interested him and he would even laugh. Major Daniel Hill, wrote this about him: "While he was always childlike and simple he possessed great originality..."[10] But when his friends mentioned it to others, they were met with disbelief. To the town at large, Jackson was an object of ridicule.[11]

Jackson had another social problem; he could not stay awake. He used to fall asleep in church, during lectures, at the Franklin Society meetings, and even during the war when some subordinate reported to him. People said that the only time he did not fall asleep was when a hypnotist visited Lexington and Jackson offered himself for demonstration. On that occasion a young Lexington lady was heard to remark: "It takes Reverend White's sermon to put Major Jackson to sleep."[12]

Whether Jackson realized people made fun of him, and paid no attention to it, or whether he did not know, is hard to tell. He enjoyed going to parties. To his sister, he wrote in spring of 1853, "I am invited to a large party and among the scramble, expect to come in for my share of fun."[13] As a bachelor, he also used to call on Lexington's young ladies. "He was an ardent admirer of true womanhood," wrote Anna Jackson, "and he had his friendships among ladies who could appreciate him."[14] The Lexington parties did not include dancing, or card playing, as this was considered then ungodly and immoral by the good members of the Presbyterian church; however, music and singing were popular.

Jackson also became friendly with John Blair Lyle, a bachelor and owner of one of the town's bookstores, who was the director of the Presbyterian Church choir. Lyle's bookshop was as much a literary salon as a place of business, and Jackson met many local citizens there. There are records that Jackson attended Bible Society meetings, went to lectures, and saw a touring company performing in druid costumes playing on ox-horn instruments. In his own way, he enjoyed himself.

His active religious phase started shortly after he came to Lexington. He was introduced to the Presbyterian church by the Hills as well as by Lyle. In a typically Jacksonian way, he became interested in the church after he borrowed a Presbyterian catechism from Hill, read it, and found it a model of brevity and conciseness - it reminded him of military orders. Although he had doubts about some of the Presbyterian doctrines, such as predestination and infant baptism, after talking it over with Lyle and Rev. White, he joined the Lexington Presbyterian Church in November 1851.[15] In the church, he became active as a Sunday school teacher and later a deacon. His church membership was perhaps the most important part of his life, but he was never particularly doctrinaire, he believed that other Christian denominations were just as good.

To guide him in his daily behavior, Jackson studied and followed G.H. Hervey's "Principles of Courtesy." These were meant to "illustrate and enforce the duty of Christian courtesy," and this appealed to his orderly mind. He seemed to find comfort in contemplating such homilies as: "Never yawn in church," or "Never place your hat in the aisle, if there is room for it in the pew," and " When you happen to be in your seat some time before service, abstain from bows, shaking hands, congratulating, talking, whispering, or gazing curiously or vacantly round the room." That he paid serious attention to it can be deduced from his heavy underlining of the text.[16]

In religion as in military matters, Jackson was happy in an authoritarian framework.[17] He did not believe in bending the rules. He demonstrated this in his observance of the Sabbath. Jackson found it distressing that the post office did not observe the Sabbath and moved the mails on Sunday. To avoid contributing to such desecration, he never picked up his letters on Sunday. He also mailed his own letters early in the week so that they would arrive at their destination by the end of the week and not be in transit on the Sabbath. During his engagement to Mary Anna Morrison, who became his second wife, she too followed this pattern.

And so it happened that one Sunday morning, as Jackson was leaving the church, a friend asked him: "I hear that you have a letter from Mary Anna." Jackson replied: "Yes, I have it here in my pocket." "Did you read it?" asked the friend. Jackson's reply was: "Assuredly not. The letter came last night, and today is Sunday. I'll read it Monday." Of course, he refused to read it Saturday evening in artificial light because he felt it was bad for his eyes, and reading one's fiancee's letter was not a suitable occupation for Sabbath, which was a day when, "one should abstain from every thought, word, and action which affords gratification to a worldly mind." The friend wondered how Jackson could concentrate on the religious service and sermon, but Jackson later said that "His tranquility and spiritual enjoyment were unusually great that day."[18]

During the Civil War, observing the Sabbath became often a problem. There were a few times when Jackson refrained from advancing or taking military action because it fell on Sunday, sometimes with serious consequences, and when he took action, he felt uncomfortable.

Jackson's military approach to religion made him report to his pastor, Dr. White, about his spiritual life and activities as he would report to a commanding officer. This surprised and perhaps alarmed dear Dr. White. He was not sure how to respond when Jackson "came for his orders and reported his performance of them" in a military way. But he appreciated the younger man's sincerity. Actually Anna Jackson also commented that her husband liked to report to her in the same manner about domestic matters.[19]

It was Major Hill who introduced Jackson to Miss Elinor Junkin, one of eight children of the president of Washington College. She and her older sister Margaret, known as Maggie, were popular members of the Lexington society. They were also active in the Presbyterian church. One day, after he had been living in Lexington for a while, Tom came to Hill's office, and after a rambling introduction, he asked Hill's advice about his strange feelings about Ellie, "I don't know what has come over me. I used to think her plain, but now I find her face all sweetness." Hill burst into laughter and told him he was obviously in love. Jackson sounded surprised but thoughtfully mentioned that he had never felt like this before, and perhaps that was what it was.[20]

Ellie was a spirited, outgoing young woman. She was described as less shy than her sister Margaret, and "she had also more pretensions to beauty, and was of merrier, more social disposition." Ellie's family as well as most of the citizens of Lexington wondered, "How such a grave and formal person as Major Jackson should captivate a girl whose vivacity and beauty had brought her many other lovers."[21] After a sometimes stormy engagement, Tom and Ellie were married on August 4, 1853. Tom was twenty-nine years old, Ellie one year younger.

A charming story is told about Tom's and Ellie's wedding day: Ellie wanted to keep their wedding plans secret and told Tom so. One morning that summer of 1853, Tom unexpectedly returned from his summer vacation and went to call on Mrs. Hill and her younger sisters, Mary Anna and Eugenia Morrison, who were visiting Lexington from North Carolina. Tom was cheerful, "He spent an hour or more calling for his favorite songs...but not even a hint did he give us as to the object of his return, although we plied him with all sorts of teasing questions," wrote Anna in her memoirs. That afternoon, he and Ellie were married. It was a simple wedding performed by Rev. Junkin, the bride's father. The ladies learned about the marriage the next day - "We were electrified next morning at hearing that he and Miss Ellie Junkin were married,"- after the young couple had left on their honeymoon.[22] Tom's sister Laura did not hear about the marriage either, until after the fact, which displeased her deeply. To punish Tom, she did not answer his letters until six months later.

They went for their honeymoon to Niagara Falls, but not alone, Ellie's sister Maggie Junkin went with them. Afterwards, they settled down into two rooms at Ellie's parents house on the Washington College campus, and Tom finally found a warm, happy family life. The Junkin family soon accepted Jackson as one of their own, and he returned their affection. But this happiness did not last long. In October 1854, Ellie bore a stillborn child and died.

They had been married just over a year. Tom was devastated. He had loved the cheerful, outgoing Ellie with all his heart.

Ellie's death hit Jackson hard. Day after day, he went to her grave, and in his letters, he even hinted at suicide. He remained living in his in-law's house, which by that time had shrunk to just Jackson's father-in-law, Dr. Junkin, and Ellie's older sister, Maggie. Mrs. Junkin had died the previous spring and the other children were away. During this period, Jackson and Maggie became very close, and every evening at nine o'clock, Maggie used to come to his rooms "for an hour or two of relaxation and chat."[23] Maggie was a highly intelligent woman, a poet, and they had much in common. Many people wondered if there was a romantic attachment between them, and if they got along so well, why they didn't marry. Perhaps the reason was that the Presbyterian church frowned on marriages between brothers- and sisters-in-law. Maggie, who was then thirty-seven years old, married someone else. A few weeks after Jackson's second wedding, she married another VMI professor, J.T.L. Preston, a widower with seven children, nine years older than herself.

Much information about Jackson comes to us from Maggie. Even after Jackson's marriage to Anna, the two saw each other often, and Jackson and Maggie corresponded during the war. With the exception of his sister Laura and his brother-in-law D.H. Hill, Maggie was probably Jackson's closest friend and confidant. In later years, Maggie published several articles about Jackson, and Maggie's step-daughter, Elizabeth Preston Allan, wrote a charming book of reminiscences about Lexington and Jackson, using Maggie's private journals. This book touches indirectly on the subject of Maggie's romantic feelings, saying that the reason why Maggie did not marry until her late thirties was that she had an "unfortunate episode in her youth, which had closed her heart."[24] Apparently, she fell in love with a young man who was not acceptable to her family. But everyone was surprised when she accepted Preston's marriage proposal because she used to say that she would never marry a widower with children as long, "as I keep my mind."[25]

JACKSON HOUSE, LEXINGTON

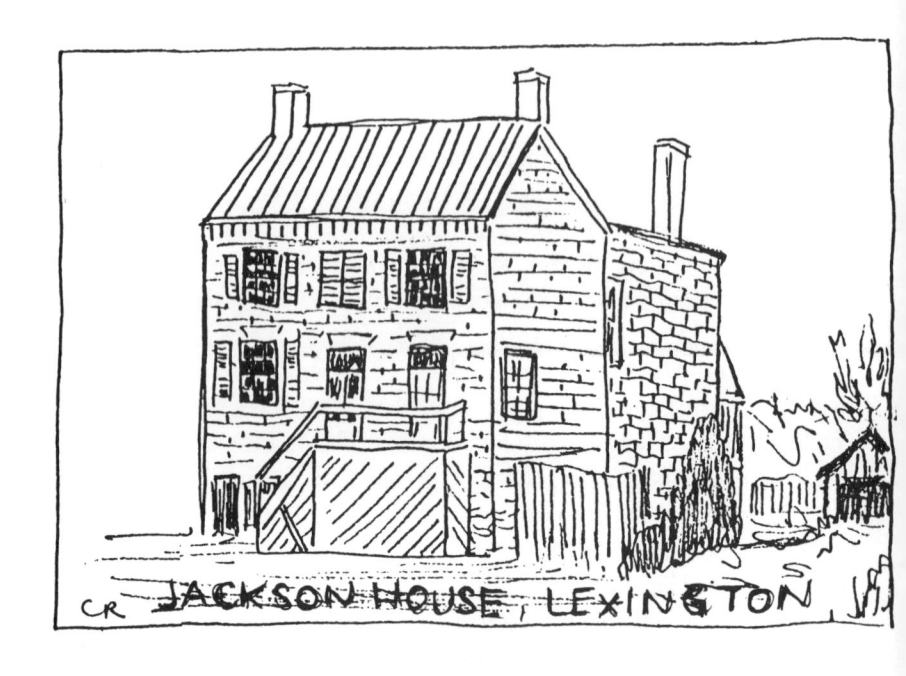

X.
SECOND MARRIAGE

In the summer of 1856, two years after Ellie's death, Jackson suddenly decided to go to Europe. He spent the previous spring planning a visit to his sister and then a trip West to purchase some land, but in the very last moment, he changed his mind - without even telling his sister. The first she heard about the European trip was in a letter written on board the ship "Asia", which was that day leaving New York for Liverpool.[1] A visit to Europe was something Jackson had wanted to do after leaving Florida, but instead he came to Lexington.

Jackson's trip lasted three months and took him through England, Belgium, France, Germany, Switzerland and Italy. Armed with guidebooks he enjoyed everything. His Scottish

Tourist Pocket Guide, A New Guide to Florence, and a Paris Guide, all heavily annotated still survive in his library. He came back "with restored health and spirits."[2] He was a changed man, he had put behind his sorrow over Ellie's death, and as his second wife delicately put it in her memoirs, "He began to realize that life could be made bright and happy to him again."[3]

With a characteristic dispatch, he wrote a letter to Miss Mary Anna Morrison, the young woman whom he saw last on the morning of his wedding day to Ellie, more than three years ago. He had not seen her since, because her sister Isabella Hill had moved to North Carolina, where D.H. Hill had taken a position at Davidson College. Davidson College had been founded by Hill's father-in-law, Dr. Morrison. Jackson wrote Anna about "the blissful memories when we had been together in Lexington,"[4] and asked if he could come and visit her at her parents home in Lincoln County, North Carolina.

Anna was perplexed by it, but not her younger sister Eugenia, "who laughed most heartily over it,"[5] and said that Major Jackson was coming courting. And so he was. Around Christmas 1856, while still living at the Junkin house, Jackson arranged a few days leave and appeared, unexpected, at the Cottage Home of the Morrisons. To everyone's surprise, except perhaps Jackson's, in two days, Mary Anna and Tom came to an agreement, and Tom left Cottage Home engaged.

Soon a wedding date was set for summer 1857, at the Morrison's home, as most everybody involved in the wedding had an academic schedule. The groomsman was Clem Fishburne, an old friend and now also professor at Davidson College. The actual date was July 16, 1857. This time, Jackson wrote a rather coy letter to his sister and invited her to the wedding, but she did not attend.[6] There were some worries about the groom arriving in time, which turned out all right, and about Anna's trousseau, ordered from New York, which almost did not make it. Also Reverend Morrison, the father of the bride, did not trust himself to perform the wedding ceremony, so another clergyman, Dr.

Drury Lacey, chaplain to Davidson College was asked. Finally on the oppressively hot day of the wedding, it was found that the groom did not post the $500 marriage bond, and the future father-in-law had to rush off on horseback to the county seat, Lincolnton, to take care of it.[7]

But it was a nice wedding, small and intimate as they were then in fashion. The guests noticed that Dr. Lacey seemed to place a special emphasis on asking the groom to be a "loving and indulgent husband,"[8] perhaps reflecting the lingering concern of the Morrison family about their new member. The Morrisons were a large, warm, close family and did not quite know what to make of this taciturn man, but they needn't have worried. Tom and Anna's marriage turned out to be a happy one. The young couple left on a honeymoon - this differed from Jackson's first one in that they did not bring along a companion, but just like last time, the destination was Niagara Falls.

In August, Jackson returned to Lexington and his teaching duties at VMI. Housing being in short supply, they lived for a while at the best hotel in town and later in a boarding house which was less expensive and gave them more privacy; however, what they wanted was a house of their own. Jackson said: "I shall never be content until I am at the head of an establishment in which my friends can feel at home in Lexington."[9]

This they found in the winter of 1858. It was an older house, and much larger than they needed, but it was a home. Jackson was delighted to have his "house with golden hinges," and a "place for everything and everything in its place."[10] They started to furnish their home with the most modern pieces of furniture, they could find. Jackson took active interest in selecting the furniture, and in his letters to Laura, he debated the advantages and disadvantages of the different styles and which furniture galleries were better than others.

The Jacksons' life in Lexington was governed by firm rules, nothing in it was ever out of place, and Jackson was a stickler for

SECOND MARRIAGE

punctuality. "His personal habits were systematic in the extreme,"[11] Anna wrote, but fortunately, she did not mind it and cheerfully accommodated her husband's routine. She wrote: "In his household the law of love reigned...his sternest rebuke was to say, ...:'Ah, that is not the way to be happy!' "[12]

Every morning, Jackson rose at 6 a.m., prayed, and summer or winter, took a cold bath in a small, round, tin bathtub. He said it was good for his circulation. This was followed by a brisk walk, in rain or shine, and he returned "looking the picture of freshness and animation," as Anna wrote in her memoirs. At 7 o'clock sharp, there were family prayers in the dining room, attended by all family members, including the servants. Anyone arriving even a few seconds after the doors were closed had to wait outside, even his wife.[13] After this came breakfast. His classes at VMI started at 8 a.m. and were finished by 11 a.m., when he returned home. Standing up at his special desk, so that all his internal organs were in alignment, he read his Bible and studied his lecture notes until dinner was served at 1 p.m.

Maggie Junkin Preston wrote: "His habits of study were peculiar and never relaxed except in illness. He would rise in the midst of the most enlivening conversation, if the appointed hour had struck, and go to his study . . . at night, with his green silk eye shade over his eyes, standing at his desk, neither paper nor book before him, he would spend hours in mentally digesting his material."[14]

When not at artillery practice with the cadets, Jackson spent the afternoons gardening, taking Anna for a carriage ride, or in exercise - as Anna wrote "..when he had a home of his own he provided himself with some of his favorite appliances for gymnastic exercises." Jackson had a garden in back of the house and a somewhat rocky twenty acre farm just outside Lexington where he grew most of the vegetables used in the household.[15] They also had two cows and some chickens. The chickens sometimes used to get loose in the garden by the house, so Jackson built a fence to keep them out. In February 1861, he reported to Anna in a letter that, "Pursuant to orders, looking into the nests, he found nine fresh eggs."[16]

In the evening, there was another religious service, especially on Sundays, when some servants from other houses attended. After supper, Major Jackson liked to re-review his lecture notes, but since he would not use his eyes after dark, he would recite them from memory. After his second marriage, he would do this in the parlor sitting on a chair facing a wall. Anna did not enjoy this part of the evening much, but when he turned back to her "with a bright and cheerful face,"[17] she was a happy woman. In her memoirs, she mentioned how they read together Shakespeare and other books, she doing the reading, he listening, studied together "Shorter Catechism" until they knew it by heart, and how she would play the piano and sing. Her husband found this especially enjoyable, despite his well known tone deafness, often even breaking into a short jig. "In the privacy of his home, he frequently used to dance the polka for exercise, but no eye but that of his wife was ever permitted to witness this recreation,"[18] wrote Anna, making sure that no one thought her husband would dance from any but the most innocent and moral reasons.

In Lexington, Jackson continued to suffer from various illnesses. In most of his letters to sister Laura, he remarked on health, both his and hers, mentioning either that he was feeling unwell or that his health was improving. The only time when health was not mentioned was during the period of April 1853, through October 1854, before and during his marriage to Ellie, when he wrote on more general topics. After Ellie's death, he went through a depression, which lifted with his marriage to Mary Anna Morrison. But four months later, in December 1857, he wrote to Laura, "Because of inflammation of the tube leading to the ear, and also inflammation of the throat (chronic), and very painful neuralgia, I have been constrained to give up my correspondence for a while. I am now compelled to use a vial of chloroform liniment per day externally, and also using internally a preparation of ammonia. The hearing of my right ear is impaired...the eye medicine helped me for a while."[19]

Jackson consulted physicians, both in Lexington and elsewhere and, in addition, almost every summer he visited some hydropathic establishment, i.e. a spa. Spas and water cures were immensely popular in those days, and the area around Lexington was especially blessed with them. Some twelve miles from Lexington was Rockbridge Baths and a few more miles west, Alum Springs. In the vicinity were Warm Springs, Hot Springs and White Sulphur Springs. If this wasn't enough, there were springs up and down the East coast, each promising relief from everything starting with dandruff and ending with fallen arches and all in between. For instance, the Bath Alum Springs were being recommended by medical authorities for scrofulous, eruptive and dyspeptic affections, as well as hepatic derangements, nervous debility and uterine diseases.

For Jackson, this was a bonanza. Almost every summer vacation during his years in Lexington, he spent at least a part of it in some spa. He took it very seriously, giving himself up to the regime of drinking the waters, bathing in them, doing the recommended exercises and writing about it in detail to sister Laura or later to Anna. In 1852, still as a bachelor, Jackson went to Alum Springs. He wrote to Laura that the place was so popular and crowded, "I succeeded in procuring half a bed, there being one room for four occupants. Though we have had but two beds to four persons, the beds are good and the servants attentive. Boarding is ten dollars per week. This water I consider is water of waters. My appetite and digestion have already improved, and I indulge rather freely." In a P.S. he added: "This establishment was sold a few days since for one hundred and fifty thousand dollars."[20] After his return home to Lexington, he remarked again and again how the waters had helped him, and in October, he mentioned that he weighed 172 lbs, which was more than six pounds over his former weight.

During their honeymoon, Jackson took Anna to Rockbridge

Alum Springs on recommendation of Dr. Graham from Lexington. Anna had an enlarged neck gland. Next summer, they were in New York, where Jackson was having his tonsils treated ("the physician says, right tonsil is inflamed towards lungs — will pare off part tomorrow")[21] and the following summer, he went to the White Sulphur Springs to cure a liver problem, which he thought was caused by his infected throat and tonsils. In addition, Jackson also used to complain of nervousness. His friend Daniel Hill confirmed it, but did not consider it incapacitating, not even in a battle: "The muscles of his face would twitch convulsively when a battle was about to open, and his hand would tremble so that he could not write. This only indicated weak nerves and not timidity. Although his nervous system was weak, he gloried in battle."[22]

Jackson also visited hydropathic establishments in Brattleboro, Vermont, and Northampton, Massachusetts, where he was treating a bilious attack and fever. Anna remained there after his departure to continue her own treatment. Jackson always felt that a stay in a spa helped him. Anna was not so sure for herself. She said that "she went to Northampton without a particle of faith into hydropathy," but that she was pleased with the results. She went there unable to walk even a mile, and after couple of months, she was walking five miles a day with ease.[23]

Another time Anna described how Jackson came back at the end of the summer ready to return to VMI. The first day of school he brought out his uniform jacket - at VMI professors as well as students wear uniforms - and was unable to button it over his chest. Through his summer health regime, his chest and shoulders became so muscular and much bigger that the old uniform did not fit. What did they do then? Did he have a larger coat, could they move the buttons? Alas, Anna did not report on how she coped with that emergency, only that he had to get a new coat made.[24]

In Lexington, Jackson continued with his diets, he still liked his food plain and mostly vegetarian. He would eat meat, but said that once or twice a week was enough. He never smoked and also avoided stimulants such as tea or coffee and drank them sparingly, saying that water was better. And he never ate between meals. If he was offered some refreshments while visiting friends, he would not touch them, "even to save social embarrassment or the feelings of his hostess," said his wife Anna.[25]

What he enjoyed was growing his own vegetables in the garden behind their house and at their small farm outside of the town. One year he grew celery, lima beans, snap beans, carrots, parsnips, salsify, onions, cabbage, turnips, beets, potatoes and muskmelons. He provided his family with more vegetables than they could use. In one of his letters to Anna (who was then getting medical treatment in the North), Jackson mentioned putting by ninety-nine heads of cabbages. In another letter, he wrote about hoeing turnips, hilling celery and, "I was in the kitchen last night to seal some jars of tomatoes.."[26] The previous spring, he reported that their cow had a calf and that he was eating lettuce from their hot-bed, which is what they called the cold frame. Gardening in those days was not always easy; seeds were hard to come by. In his correspondence with sister Laura, Jackson often mentioned trying to find some seeds for her or apologizing that he was unable to do so.

Anna, in common with most of the Southern ladies of that time, did not concern herself much with domestic duties, these were handled by the servants - Negro slaves actually - but they were always called servants. Owning slaves did not seem to bother Jackson, he was used to it. When he was a youngster at the Jackson Mill his uncle Cummins had slaves. Tom thought of them as members of the family. He called one of them Uncle Jack Robinson. In 1850, in a letter to his sister, he reported that Uncle Jack and Aunt Nancy were dead (both "colored slaves" according to a note by Tom Arnold), in the same sentence and in the same manner as reporting about his blood relatives.[27]

In his early teens, Jackson discussed slavery with his friend Joe Lightburn. The boys decided that the Negroes should be free and even be taught to read so that they could study the Bible.[28] Incidentally, just about that time Tom taught one of his uncle Cummins' Negroes to read and write. Then the man wrote himself a pass and escaped on the underground railway north.[29]

When Jackson was living in Lexington, he had two slaves. His second wife Mary Anna brought him three more as her dowry; they were Hetty, Anna's old nurse and her teen-aged sons Cyrus and George. Jackson acquired one of his slaves, Albert, because the man wanted to buy his freedom. He asked Major Jackson to buy him and then rent him out to various hotels or to work at VMI and to apply the wages toward his freedom. Albert did not live at the house except if he became ill. He did get his freedom at the beginning of the war, although Mrs. Jackson believed that his freedom fund did not cover it fully.[30] She was most likely right; Albert's wages at Rockbridge Alum Springs were $15 a month, or $180 a year, and they were probably comparable at the other places where he worked, so it would have taken ten years or more to earn the $2,000 at which he was probably valued.

The next servant was old Amy who was to be sold for debt when Jackson bought her. At that time, he was a widower without his own household, so he did not have any use for her. However Amy begged him to buy her. According to Mrs. Jackson, her husband arranged "a home for her in a good Christian family, until he had one of his own." After his marriage to Anna, "She proved her gratitude by serving him faithfully." Mrs. Jackson adds, "She was one of the best colored cooks, and was a real treasure to me in my new experience as a housekeeper."[31] When Amy could work no longer, this being during the Civil War, Jackson arranged for her to stay with a free black woman and paid for her keep and later funeral. When he received news about her death, " the tears came to my eyes more than once while reading it," he wrote to Anna.[32]

A little girl Emma he also bought from compassion, with

SECOND MARRIAGE

the hope that she would grow up to be Anna's personal maid. Emma was only four years old, and Jackson bought her when she was orphaned and no one wanted her. He did it during Anna's absence from Lexington. "On my return he took great pleasure in surprising me with this new present, which, by the way, proved rather troublesome,"[33] wrote Anna in her memoirs.

While Jackson was living in Lexington, he often worked side by side with his Negroes in his fields, twenty acres, where he raised vegetables for the family's use. Although small farmers would work alongside their slaves, this was not a universal habit. When Jackson was a youngster, he was reminded of it by a family friend, Colonel Withers, who said, "Gentlemen have servants for such tasks and work with their heads instead of their hands."[34] But Jackson thought nothing of it. He was an enthusiastic gardener and enjoyed physical work.

Jackson felt responsible for his servants both in the physical and spiritual sense. He started a hugely successful Colored Sunday School, where he taught for many years. Other people who tried it before had failed, but Jackson had as many as a hundred students each Sunday, and they kept coming back - despite the fact that Jackson started each class by singing a hymn. It was always the same hymn, "Amazing Grace," and Jackson was notorious for his tin ear and dismal voice. One man said about his singing that braying of a donkey would have been better.

At home he asked Anna to teach his Negroes to read the Bible, even though this was against the law.[35] During the Civil War, he continued to worry about his servants. He wrote to a Lexington friend who was taking care of them, "My boys should be able to attend the colored Sabbath-school in Lexington...as I am very desirous that the spiritual interests of my servants shall be attended to." When one of Hetty's sons, Cyrus, asked permission to be married, Jackson reported to his wife that he would give his consent provided she and Cy's mother did not object.

Jackson was a soldier, he carried policies out, he did not

make them. This probably shaped his opinion on slavery; as a Virginian, slavery to him was a fact of life. Basically, he believed that slaves should be freed, but he did not believe it could be done quickly.[36] Whatever discomfort he may have felt about slavery was lessened when he assured himself that the Bible did not prohibit it and that Negroes, both slaves and free, could be saved and enter the gates of Heaven. According to his wife, "He found the institution of slavery a responsible and troublesome one - but he believed that the Bible taught that slavery was sanctioned by the Creator himself, who maketh men to differ and instituted laws for the bound and the free," and, " I am very confident that he would never have fought for the sole object of perpetuating slavery. It was for her constitutional rights that the South resisted the North."[37]

Jackson had a finely honed feel for money matters, perhaps because there had been so little of it in his early years. He never earned a great deal, but he usually saved a good part of his salary. This he later invested in stocks that gave him a small interest. When he was in the US Army, Jackson earned between $85 and $150 a month, or $1,020 to $1,800 a year. When he started teaching at the Virginia Military Institute, he was paid $1,200 per year, which, over the years, went up to $1,350. During the Civil War, his pay as a brigadier general was $300 a month plus an additional $100, but at that time, this would not buy a great deal, as prices of everything went up. In comparison, the pay of a Confederate private was $11 a month in 1863, which was raised to $18 the next year. The Union privates received $16, but this was in gold value, so their buying power was much greater.

In 1856, when he had been at VMI for five years, Jackson thought of buying about two or three thousand acres of land in the West. "I desire to employ all my spare funds in the purchase of lands," he wrote to his sister in June. But eventually, he decided against it, because he was afraid that, in case of a war between free and slave states, he might lose it. According to Jackson, this land was selling at about one dollar an acre. This

SECOND MARRIAGE

suggests that he saved almost half of the salary that he received since he came to Lexington.[38]

In letters to his sister Laura, finances were frequently mentioned. Often it was a matter of buying something for her in New York City, or Philadelphia, such as clothing, books, wine or even furniture. At other times, there were sums owed to family friends or relatives which she was to pay for him. And for a long time, there were matters to do with their half-brother Wirt, who was something of a black sheep of the family. In 1855, Jackson offered to give Wirt one thousand dollars to buy a farm, but not trusting him, he set conditions on it; one of their uncles would have to approve the selection, and the land must not cost more than seven dollars an acre. The purchase of the farm did not go through, but in February 1857, Jackson was writing Laura about lending "two or four hundred dollars for Wirt to buy stock to drive to California." Jackson's comment was: "I do not have the money, but even if I had, should not have lent it, I do not approve of Wirt going to California," but he was willing to send him a small sum later.[39]

In Lexington, Jackson helped to establish a bank and became a director. This was the first bank in Rockbridge County. It was much needed. Before banks were common, sending money from place to place was difficult. Often one had to depend on the willingness and honesty of travelers, who would take the money with them and deliver it at the other end. The safety of this method was doubtful, so often people would send just one half of a torn bill in a letter and then later the other half, and the recipient would paste it together.

Jackson also bought a one third interest in a leather tannery, and with his second wife Anna, he bought a handsome brick house. The price of the house was $3,000 and it is possible that the Jacksons spent part of Anna's dowry on it . Her father had given her five or six slaves upon her marriage, and Jackson kept only three of them, selling the others (possibly to Anna's brother, because Rev. Morrison felt that slaves should be kept together and in the family). [40] This would have covered the cost of the house. But furnishing the house stretched the family resources. In a letter to Laura the following August, Jackson mentioned that he had to borrow money to get along, because of the house.[41]

To furnish their home, the Jacksons bought the best furniture they could afford - simple but elegant. In their house on Washington Street, they had three stoves - a kitchen stove and two parlor stoves - when most people were still using fireplaces to heat and to cook. They even had a piano, which in an inventory made after Jackson's death was valued at $500. He and Anna did their furniture shopping in New York or Philadelphia, mostly because the selection, styles, and possibly even the prices were better than in Lexington. In the case of a sofa, which they bought at an auction, this did not work out. Perhaps they got carried away at the auction, as it tends to happen, but when the sofa arrived in Lexington, Major Jackson was disappointed. He wrote to his sister that the green sofa arrived and "that he feared they had been cheated." [42]

Jackson knew how to spend money on things which mattered to him. From his first army salary at West Point, he bought a dress for his sister Laura. While in Mexico, he purchased a first class horse. When he was stationed in New York, he acquired a small but good library,[43] and every summer he traveled. He even took an extensive tour of Europe. The European tour was most likely financed by the funds originally meant for land purchase in the West. And from the time he joined the Presbyterian church, Jackson tithed at least one tenth of his salary.[44]

Jackson took his financial obligations to the church very seriously. Right after the bloody, first battle of Manassas, (which gave him his name Stonewall), wounded on his hand, Jackson sent a letter to his pastor. When this letter arrived in Lexington, the church congregation was eager to hear a first hand report from the front. As Reverend White opened the letter and read it to the assembled people they heard: "My dear pastor, in my tent last night, after a fatiguing day's service, I remembered that I had failed to send you my contribution for our Colored Sunday-school. Enclosed you will find my check for that object, which please acknowledge at your earliest convenience, and oblige yours faithfully, T. J. Jackson."[45]

At the beginning of the war, Jackson sold his small farm and other investments and put it all into Confederate bonds. During the war, he wrote to his wife that he was sending her $1,000, no doubt his pay, to be invested in Confederate bonds, "...as far as possible, persons should take Confederate bonds, so as to relieve the government from any pecuniary pressure." She was not to cash in the coupons, because they were paid in gold and, "Citizens should not receive a cent of gold from the government when it is so scarce."[46]

XI.
TO ARMS

Although born and bred Virginian, Jackson was too much a professional soldier to join the Southern cause without soul searching. He did not speak up on the issue in public, but privately he hoped that the Union was going to survive. In December 1860, he was writing to his sister, Laura, "I am strong for the Union at present, and if things become no worse I hope to continue so..."[1] and in February 1861, he said he was going to vote for the Union candidates for the State Convention. When he was asked whether or not the South should fight for its rights, he agreed, but said that it can do so better as part of the Union.[2]

However, once the first shots were fired, Jackson did not vacillate. Speaking to the VMI cadets on April 13, 1861, he said that military men should make short speeches, and come to the point. "The time for war has not yet come, but it will come, and that soon; and when it does come, my advice is to draw the sword and throw away the scabbard." Virginia seceded on April 17.

In Virginia, which was a border state, this wasn't just a war between the states it was often between friends and family members. In Jackson's case, the first such break came with his former father-in-law Reverend Dr. George Junkin, whom he admired deeply. In 1861, the Pennsylvania-born Junkin resigned his position as president of Washington College in Lexington, and left the town, because he did not believe that Virginia should secede.

Jackson's sister Laura Arnold lived in the western part of the state, which became West Virginia. She later became a Union sympathizer, although apparently her husband was for the Confederacy. During the war, Laura was active in nursing wounded soldiers, and a contemporary report quotes her as saying: "I can take care of Federal soldiers as fast as Thomas would wound them."[3] How much Jackson knew about Laura's war-time activities is uncertain, but there is no record that he wrote her after the start of the war.

On April 21, 1861, Jackson with a detachment of VMI cadets, left for Richmond and the war. His departure from Lexington was typical. The detachment was to leave at one o'clock. Jackson had arranged for Rev. White to offer a prayer to send them on their way. Fifteen minutes were allotted for this ceremony, but the minister finished sooner. Everyone expected an order to start marching, but Major Jackson pulled up a small stool and sat down. As the minister and the troops waited in tense silence, an officer came and said: "Everything is now ready, may we start?", but Major Jackson just pointed at the Institute clock. After five minutes, the clock boomed the hour. At the last stroke of it, Major Jackson stood up and his sharp command rang out: "Forward, march!"[4]

When he arrived in Richmond with the VMI cadets, one

observer wrote about him: "His blue forage cap sat back on his head, and he stood like a horse sprung at the knees," and "His orders to the students were given in a piping whining tone."[5] Although others were getting exalted ranks, with Mexican War records frequently used to justify them, Jackson's Mexican accomplishments were totally ignored. Where others were getting commands of troops, Jackson's first assignment was at the rank of Major, the same as he had at VMI, to a desk job drawing maps. He hated engineering, and the rank was an insult.[6]

A few days later, his name came up in the State Convention in Richmond for another assignment, but the first response was: "But who is this Major Jackson?" Fortunately, a Rockbridge delegate spoke up: "He is the one who, if you order him to hold a post, will never leave it alive to be occupied by the enemy."[7] Subsequently, Jackson received his assignment as colonel of the line.

Then came the hard work. With the same dogged determination of his West Point days, he harried and shaped his men into fighting machines. At first his men resented him, he made them work too hard, but as soon as the first skirmishes came, they saw the point of it, and he earned their grudging admiration. Once the war started, Jackson's meteoric rise and military success were both surprising and perfectly logical: there were few lucky breaks in it, he earned it.

By the way, calling the Union army Bluecoats and the Confederates Grays was not always accurate. Not only because at times Stonewall Jackson himself wore his old blue uniform coat, and many of the Confederate soldiers wore whatever they could find, which sometimes were blue military tunics of their dead enemies, but also there were a number of Federal units whose uniforms were gray with black piping - the same as the Confederates: The 3rd New York, 1st Vermont and almost all Indiana troops, units from Maine, Kansas and Nebraska all wore gray uniforms as the war started. Conversely, the uniforms of the Rockbridge Artillery, from Lexington, among others, were blue.

Not surprisingly, this caused confusion and accidents. Eventually, the Union command tried to provide blue uniforms for all their soldiers, but these were not always appreciated, they were lighter and not as well made as what the soldiers brought with them from home.

Jackson earned his name Stonewall on the Manassas battlefield on July 21, 1861, where he was with his First Brigade. This battle is also known as Bull Run. Manassas was what the Confederates called it. Bull Run was the Federal name. Many of the Civil War battles are known under two names; the reason for this is that the Confederates being local people called battles by the names of their towns or villages, while the Union troops, not knowing the area, used the names of rivers which they found on their maps.

That day, the outnumbered Confederate forces, fighting against General McDowell's troops, were being pushed back. General Bee of South Carolina was trying to rally his troops with little success. He rode up to Jackson and said: "General, they are beating us back." "Then, Sir, we will give them the bayonet," replied Jackson coldly. General Bee galloped back to his troops and shouted at his two thousand panicking men: "Look at Jackson, standing there like a stone wall. Rally behind the Virginians!" That in the confusion of the battle this exhortation was heard and heeded is as amazing as that the name survived into history. Its author, however, did not even survive the battle: General Bernard E. Bee was killed the same day.[8]

There is some question whether General Bee's shout meant that he was encouraged by Jackson's offer of help or that he was annoyed that Jackson was standing there and not doing something. Obviously, we will never know, but the usual interpretation is the first one.

Still, some twenty years later Jackson's friend and brother-in-law, Daniel Hill, wrote an article for the Century Magazine, where he said that the Stonewall incident may not have even happened. Hill said that a reporter during the Mexican war wrote that General Zachary Taylor was called by his troops "Old Rough and Ready" despite the fact no one in the army had heard about it before, "but it struck the public's fancy and earned him several thousand votes for the presidency." Hill said that much the same thing happened with Stonewall, "Not only was the tale a sheer fabrication, but the name was least suited to Jackson, who was ever in motion, sweeping like an eagle on his prey."[9]

The first battle at Manassas gave Jackson a name, but it did not make him an instant hero. General Beauregard got most of the credit. Jackson's wife felt that he had been slighted by the press, but her husband wrote her that "my brigade is not a brigade of newspaper correspondents."[10]

Little Sorrel, Stonewall Jackson's horse, also started gaining fame. Eventually, he became almost as famous as General Lee's Traveller. Except that Little Sorrel was not an imposing horse, he was much like his master - calm, dependable and hardy. Jackson found him early in 1861 at Harper's Ferry, when he was in charge of supplies for the troops. His men "impressed" a B & O train, and there was this small sorrel horse which Jackson thought would be just right for his wife Anna. So he bought him. He did not confiscate him without a payment but paid the quartermaster what he judged to be a fair price.[11]

As it happened, Anna did not get her horse because the general became attached to him. Little Sorrel carried General Jackson through the whole Valley Campaign, except for a short period when he had been lost or stolen. Jackson's men remembered the general riding Sorrel while asleep, "He nodded and swayed through the night ride. The staff watched in fascination, but he always righted himself." Once a soldier did not recognize the general and called out to him: "I say, old fellow, where the devil did you get your liquor?" When the soldier came closer and saw who the "old fellow" was, he quickly skittered away into the darkness. But Jackson wasn't offended, he thought it was funny.[12]

Some people described Little Sorrel as being a gaunt horse but Mrs. Jackson in her memoirs disagrees. She says he was a fat horse, and although General Jackson had other, more handsome mounts, he rode him in most of the battles because he found his gait "as easy as the rocking of a cradle."[13] Today, one can see Little Sorrel in Lexington; not alive of course, he has been stuffed and is displayed in the VMI Museum.

XII.
FAMILY LIFE IN WAR

Anna, like most women through the ages, did not show the same zeal for war as her husband. She wanted her husband home, and if this wasn't possible, she wanted to be with him wherever he was. This was not a totally unreasonable request. Officers did take leave to tend to affairs at home, and many wives were able to visit husbands in the field. But Jackson's stern feeling for duty made it difficult. In this respect, he was especially harsh, he refused to give his men leave, even in cases of family emergency, and he never took one himself.

Once an officer asked for an extension of his leave because he was desperately needed at home; his father had died and another family member was on the brink of death. General Jackson responded with a letter saying : ". . . I wish I could relieve your sorrowing heart. From me you have a friend's sympathy. . But we must think of the living. . . . It is necessary that you should be at your post immediately. Join me tomorrow morning."[1]

Jackson certainly would not leave his men, ever. Although Anna was lonely in Lexington and wanted to see him home or join him, he wrote her: "My darling, I cannot be absent from my command. . . . I ought not to see my esposita, as it might make the troops feel that they were badly treated and that I consult my own pleasure and comfort regardless of theirs."[2] So Anna decided to close their house in Lexington, where she did not have any family, and return to her parents in North Carolina.

But she still wanted to see him. In her letters she kept up her requests, and he was softening: "I wish my sweet darling could be with me now . . enjoy the sweet music of the brass band of the Fifth Regiment."[3] Finally, in September 1861, he agreed to her visit at Manassas. It turned out to be an adventure. In the custom of the times, Anna was expected to travel accompanied by some gentleman, but she lost her escort in Richmond. The last leg of the trip, she had to travel alone in a train full of soldiers. When she arrived at Manassas, Jackson was nowhere to be seen. She continued one more stop to Fairfax, which was supposed to have a large military establishment, but no one was there either. She spent the night locked in her train carriage. The next day, an acquaintance went over to a nearby military hospital and arranged for a room for her. It was there that Jackson found her soon afterwards. He arrived in an ambulance, and this being Sunday, he took her first to a church service for the troops.

For the next two weeks, Anna was able to stay in a room at a local farmer's home. She ate with Jackson at the staff mess table and had a grand time, especially since Jackson's headquarters tent was right outside in the farmyard. Her husband took her to see the scene of the battle at Manassas, where he had earned his name. Anna found the area itself unremarkable and the Bull

Run stream much smaller than she had imagined it.[4] Coincidentally, the First Manassas was fought on the day which happened to be Anna Jackson's birthday. Anna reminded her husband of it, and he assured her that after this, he was never going to forget her birthday even when he might not remember his own.[5]

Anna's second visit to her husband came in December of the same year. He had just been promoted to major general and put in charge of the entire Valley of Virginia. He wanted to share with her this proud moment and wrote her: " I hope to have my little dove with me this winter,"[6] and later, "I have much work to perform, and wouldn't have much time to talk to my darling except at night; but then there is so much pleasant society among the ladies here that you could pass your time very agreeably."[7] His headquarters were in Winchester, and there Anna joined him.

Winchester may hold an unenviable record: during the war it changed hands seventy-six times. Jackson returned there again, but not with Anna.

Anna's trip north was again adventurous. The only escort she could find was an elderly, absentminded clergyman, who was more trouble than he was worth. He was so busy entertaining the wife of General Jackson that he forgot to watch her luggage and all of Anna's new clothes and gifts for her husband became lost. She arrived in Winchester in the middle of the night, and again she found no husband to welcome her. She was walking, tired and a bit dejected, up the stairs of the hotel when a man in a heavy cloak and large hat stepped forward from the crowd of uniformed figures, grabbed her in his arms and kissed her hard several times. It was Thomas. Anna chided him for not welcoming her at the doors of the stagecoach, and he laughingly replied that he wanted to be sure that he did not kiss "anyone else's esposa.." [8]

Anna was able to stay in Winchester until early March, the longest time she spent with her husband in wartime. And after much effort by her husband, even her trunk was found some three weeks later, "securely locked up in Richmond as lost baggage!"[9]

Although Jackson was certainly busy, and at times frustrated with all sorts of interference in his command coming out of Richmond, Anna's presence in Winchester made it bearable, and she indeed found the people welcoming and pleasant. They stayed with the family of a Presbyterian clergyman, Dr. Graham, where they felt very much at home. Jackson is remembered as frolicking with the Graham children and having long religious discussions with his host. All the Grahams became very fond of Tom and Anna. In later years, Dr. Graham would declare that he never saw anything strange about Jackson: "Whatever peculiarities he had were just those individual characteristics which we all in a greater or lesser degree possess."[10] This visit also had a very happy result. In late November 1862, Anna bore her second child.

Jackson's first child, with Ellie, was stillborn, however he mourned him less than his mother. Three-and-a-half years later, on April 30, 1858, Anna gave him a daughter. They named her Mary Graham after her maternal grandmother, but the baby got jaundice and died less than a month later. This loss touched Jackson deeply, but he bowed to God's will. He announced her death to his ten year old niece Grace Arnold, saying: "Did you ever think, my dear Grace, that the most persons who have died and gone to heaven are children?"[11]

This was sadly true in those days. Child mortality was appalling. There were few families not touched by it. Parents were often afraid to become attached to their children because they expected to lose them. There was a feeling that too great a love for a child was tempting fate. One can hear this in Jackson's comment on the death of a young son of the Daniel Hills. Jackson wrote to Anna, saying that he was not surprised it happened because he thought the boy's father was much too attached to him. When their daughter Julia was born, Jackson wrote to his wife: "Do not set your affections upon her, except as a gift from God," and "If she absorbs too much of our hearts, God may remove her from us."[12]

Still, his daughter's birth was a source of great happiness to Jackson. He liked children, and they liked him. It was a pity that he did not have a houseful of them. He would have made a great father. While he tended to be stiff and formal with adults, he was relaxed with children, found it easy to talk to them, and he enjoyed playing with them. During the Civil War, whenever Jackson was staying with some family, people always remarked how well he got along with the children. In Winchester at the Grahams, he was often seen romping with the children or carrying them on his shoulders.[13]

Later, while staying at Moss Neck with the Corbin family, Jackson became a great friend of their five year old daughter Janie. She used to visit him in his headquarters, sit on the floor, and the two of them would talk and play for hours. Jackson told her tales, and Janie taught the general to cut out of paper the Stonewall Brigade. One day when Janie lost her hair ribbon, Jackson cut off the gold braid from his new hat, one which Janie had always admired, and tied her hair with it, saying, "Janie, it suits a little girl like you better than it does an old soldier like me." Sadly, Janie died shortly afterwards of a fever.[14]

Throughout his life, Jackson was close to Tom and Grace and Stark, the children of his sister Laura Arnold. He wrote them frequent letters full of advice, and Tom Arnold stayed with the Jacksons in Lexington so that he could attend school there. Jackson showed great interest in his nephew's education, urging him to study Latin and learn to spell well. He encouraged Grace to study too. In one letter, he confided to her, "When I was young I committed the blunder of learning to read before I learned to spell well."[15]

Jackson's daughter was born on Sunday, November 23, 1862, at the home of Anna's sister, Mrs. Harriet Irwin, in Charlotte, North Carolina.[16] They named her Julia after Jackson's mother. "My mother was mindful of me when I was a helpless, fatherless child; and I wish to commemorate her now," he wrote to Anna when she asked him what to name the child.[17]

When Julia was born, her father did not mention the news to anyone, not even to his closest staff. They had to find out about it - weeks later - from other sources. To make sure the word wasn't going to get out, Jackson asked his wife to write him a letter rather than sending a telegram when the baby was born.[18] But when the word did get out that Stonewall became a father, the troops immediately cheered Little Stonewall. When the correction came that it was a girl, she was nicknamed Little Miss Stonewall.

At the time when Julia was born, her father was with his men near Gordonsville. There was no hope that he would join Anna and the baby. Jackson never left his men, never took a leave during the war. He would not bend this rule even to see his child. In February, he wrote Anna; "I haven't seen my wife for nearly a year, and have never seen our darling little daughter; but it is important that I, and those at headquarters, should set an example of remaining at the post of duty."[19]

Still, he very much wanted to see his daughter. In January, he wrote, "I am still thinking and thinking about that baby, and do want to see her. Can't you send her to me by express?"[20] But a newborn child (which by the way came down with chicken pox), winter, war and travel just did not seem compatible, and in spring, when the weather improved, active campaigns were likely to start. However in April, when the roads were still too wet for the campaign to resume, and the baby was a sturdy five months old, Jackson asked his wife to visit him. "I am beginning to look for my darling and my baby," and "There is no time for hesitation if you have not started,"[21] Jackson wrote Anna on April 18th she arrived on the 20th. At that time, Jackson was at Hamilton's Crossing, some five miles south of Fredericksburg. Anna, Julia and Hetty, who was now acting as Julia's nurse, arrived by train at the Guinea Station. Jackson found a room for them nearby, at the house of William Yerby.

Despite the long train ride, and the wet and rainy day, little Julia welcomed her father with her best smile. Jackson fell in love with her on the spot. When Anna said that the child took after him, he said: "No. She is too pretty to look like me."[22]

People who were with them during that time described Jackson's joy in his daughter. In the afternoon, he would come back to their room and immediately head for the crib, pick up the baby, hold her in his arms and amuse her. He talked to her, lifted her up to a mirror, saying, "Now, Miss Jackson, look at yourself!"[23] He also made a great point out of announcing how pleased he was that he had a daughter, so that people would not think he would have preferred a son.[24]

However, he was not totally indulgent with Julia: if she was crying, he did not let Anna pick her up, saying that the child had to learn discipline. He believed it was never too early for that. When the baby was only two months, he wrote Anna that he was pleased she had started disciplining the baby, and " She must not be permitted to have a will of her own." [25]

Jackson decided that the child should be baptized and the day was set for April 23, her fifth month's birthday. The chaplain, Mr. Lacey, officiated. By popular demand, Jackson invited his fellow officers to the ceremony, which was held in the front parlor of the Yerby house. Everything went well, except that the guest of honor, Julia, happened to be a bit late. The general, himself always punctual, quickly went to the other room and brought her out in his own arms.[26] Jackson's officers gave Julia a handsome silver baby cup, which still exists and is now in the Stonewall Jackson House in Lexington.

Mrs. Jackson thought that her husband looked well, especially the day when he showed her his new horse "Superior." It was a big bay horse, gift of the citizens of Augusta County. Jackson was showing off and galloped so fast that his hat fell off, but he did not even slow down. Anna later wrote that she saw in him, "the impersonation of fearlessness and manly vigor."[27]

To keep this memory fresh, Anna persuaded Jackson to have his portrait taken by a photographer from a Richmond studio who happened to be there. The general posed in the hall of the Yerby house, in a uniform coat that Jeb Stuart had given him, Anna called it "the handsome suit" - and she arranged his hair herself. There was a breeze coming through an open door which made the general frown. It gave him a look of sternness which Mrs. Jackson did not like, but this photo became a favorite of Jackson's soldiers because they thought it was most soldierly-looking.[28]

As the weather improved and roads dried out, the enemy was ready to start moving. On April 29, just nine days after Anna's arrival, a crash of cannon made it clear that General Hooker's forces were attacking. After a very brief farewell in the early morning, the general left, and Mrs. Jackson set to packing. She hoped to see him again, but the fighting was starting in earnest, and her husband could only send her a short note. Mr. Lacey, the chaplain, drove her to the train station, because neither her husband nor her brother Joseph Morrison could be spared. As she was leaving the Yerby house, she saw the first bloody casualties being brought in.[29]

XIII.

STONEWALL JACKSON'S WAY

Jackson's comrades in arms said that his favorite words were "Press on men, press on" and calls of "Close ranks" to keep the troops from straggling. Others thought that "We start at dawn," and "Let us not burn any more daylight"[1] were his favorites. But what was so different about Jackson? Why was he successful where others failed?

One long ballad with a refrain "That's Stonewall Jackson's way" speaks about "The old slouched hat cocked over his eye askew; Quick step! We're with him before morn! Bayonets and grape hear him roar....That's Banks, he is fond of shell; Lord save his soul we'll give him —well. That's Stonewall Jackson's way!"[2] Obviously, these were some of his ways; the most important was that he won battles.

General Taliaferro, who fought under him, said about Jackson, "He sought advice and counsel of none. He never called a council of war, but acted solely on his own responsibility." This was not always appreciated by his fellow officers, but the troops were more forgiving. Even in the worst moments, his men used to say: "Old Jack got us into this fix, and with the blessing of God, he will get us out."[3]

Jackson always saw the big picture. He was not one to win a battle but lose the war. Also, he was aggressive; always preferring "to attack at once, furiously,"[4] rather than wait for the enemy to do something. After the first battle of Manassas, while he was having his wound tended, he was saying, "Give me ten thousand fresh troops, and I'll march my Brigade into Washington tonight."[5] And after each battle, he wanted to do the same. He said, "Never let up in the pursuit as long as your men have strength to follow, for an army routed can be destroyed by half their number."[6]

His long suffering soldiers made fun of this. A story is told about one private grumbling: "I wish the Yankees would go to Hell." His buddy responds with, "Hell no, I don't." "And why not?" he is asked. "Well, if they did, Old Jack would make us follow them."[7] A Federal officer who had been taken prisoner by Jackson agreed with it, "Stonewall Jackson's men will follow him to the devil, and he knows it."[8]

Jackson was secretive, he would not share his plans with anyone. His aim was "to deceive and mystify the enemy." In the process, he usually also mystified his fellow Confederates. His quartermaster, John Harman, tried to resign many times because he found that "Jackson's mysterious ways were unbearable, he was a cracked man," and "the hardest master any man ever served."[9] General Whiting, sent to reinforce Jackson's forces, was so furious that the general did not brief him that he said: "I believe he hasn't any more sense than my horse."[10] But Jackson believed that "He walks with speed who walks alone." When a member of the general's staff complained about his habit of secrecy, Old Stonewall replied, "If my coat knew what I intended to do, I'd take it off and throw it away."[11]

He impressed secrecy on the men as well. Once, when the soldiers were told not to answer any questions about their movements, one of General Hood's "Texicans" was caught out of ranks, climbing a cherry tree. That was a breach of discipline which Old Jack took very seriously, and he happened to be passing by. He stopped and inquired : "Where are you going?" The man answered: "I don't know." The general, getting testier, asked: "What command do you belong to," then, "What state are you from," each time getting the same answer, "I don't know." So Jackson turned to another soldier and asked what it was all about. What he got was: "Well, yesterday old Stonewall and General Hood said that we don't know anything until the next fight. So we don't know." Jackson, who usually would have exploded, just laughed and rode on.[12]

During the second battle of Manassas, Old Jack led an army of 25,000 men over fifty miles in two days by telling his lieutenants how to march from crossroad to crossroad, without telling them their destination. The orders were: "March to a cross-road; a staff officer there will inform you which fork to take, and so to the next fork, where you will find a courier with a sealed direction pointing out the road." Every twenty minutes the column halted for two minutes - the men stacked their arms and lay down flat on their backs. "A man rests all over when he lies down,"[13] directed General Jackson. One can imagine their grumbling. But it worked. They surprised the enemy, who thought they were miles away.

Jackson was fast. He could move his men with incredible speed to attack the enemy from the side or even from the rear. Kyd Douglas said of him: "Swiftness of execution was his most popular virtue - he was the most rapid mover of the South," and his old brigade got the name of "Jackson's Foot Cavalry."[14] It was said that Jackson's men believed he could do anything he wished, and he believed that his men could do anything he commanded. His men put it more succinctly. They claimed that "Moses took forty years to bring Israelites through the wilderness. Old Jack could do it on half ration in three days."[15]

Jackson was a man of strategy. He knew how to make the enemy divide his forces so that he would have to fight only part of them - and not be badly outnumbered. This was how, during the Valley campaign, he defeated the forces of the Union generals Banks, Shields, and Fremont. In the summer of 1862 battles of Cross Keys and Port Republic, Jackson marched four hundred miles in forty days, fought four battles, defeating four separate armies, captured three thousand five hundred prisoners, killing many more, and neutralized an enemy army three times as large as his own. And while thus keeping the Union forces occupied in skirmishes in the Valley of Virginia, he kept them from taking Richmond.

Jackson knew his terrain. He used scouts, questioned local residents, found the best mapmakers and had them survey the area, and then he familiarized himself with all the roads and byways, rivers, creeks, hills and valleys. He learned all this so well that, afterwards, he never had to refer to the maps again. From his memory, he could plan strategies and attacks and direct the battles and skirmishes.

"The enemy believed he never slept," said about him his aide Kyd Douglas, "but in fact he slept a great deal. Give him five minutes to rest, he slept four and a half of them."[16] At the same time, it was always, "We must not burn any more daylight," and "We start at dawn," that is, if not before dawn, at two or three o'clock in the morning. Even in camp, he was an early riser, doing all his writing before breakfast. This was a sore point with his younger aides, who spent their evenings in social activities and liked to sleep in. But the general expected them in attendance. Before Jackson took his brother-in-law Joseph Morrison on his staff, he wrote to Anna: "If you will vouch for Joseph's being an early riser during the remainder of the war, I will give him an aide-ship."[17] She did, and Joseph stayed with Jackson until the general's death. Jackson did not live apart from his personal staff, he liked to have them around, although they were by and large much younger men. He enjoyed their vitality, their jokes, even though he did not join in it himself.

Jackson was harder on himself than on his staff. In addition to early rising, he often spent his nights conferring with other commanders. On one occasion, he rode fifty miles to meet with General Lee and then rode right back, doing it all in a day and a half, without sleep, except what he could get in the saddle. He spent his days on horseback, often slept on the bare ground in all kinds of weather, getting two or three hours of sleep a night, and his meals were spartan, that is, if he ate at all. Despite such hardships, Jackson's health during the war was remarkably good. Even his eyes improved, so he was able to read and write in the evening.

Fighting on the Sabbath was a dilemma. Jackson preferred to avoid it, if he could, but military needs came first. "I always try to keep the Sabbath if the enemy will let me," he told a member of his staff.[18] If the enemy did not let him, Jackson might agonize over it, but then he would say that the Lord was the judge - if he forgave the sinning soldier, He was going to give him victory. He always gave credit for his successes to "the kind Providence." Such complete trust in God's will gave Jackson an unshakeable confidence and an almost total freedom from any regrets. Jackson believed that "all things work together for good to them that love God."[19]

Much was made of Old Stonewall's praying - before the battle or during it - it was viewed with derision, admiration and perhaps even envy. It is said that General Richard Ewell was so impressed by Jackson's religious fervor that he said: "If this is religion, I must have it," and shortly afterwards, Ewell made a profession of faith.[20] Jackson's servant Jim used the prayers as a barometer. He said that he always knew when a big battle was near, "The general is a great man for praying, night and mornings - all times. But when I see him get up and pray several times in the night besides, then I know there is going to be something to pay; and I go straight and pack his haversack, because I know he will call for it in the morning."[21]

He paid attention to details. People laughed at him when he made his men move a score of railroad cars from the B & O shop in Martinsburg to Winchester - because he did it on roads. To do it on rails would have taken them into Union held territory. Jackson had his men push and pull the cars over land, and in one instance used a forty-horse team, so he was able to save them and use them later. Those cars he could not move, he reluctantly destroyed.

Another time, Old Jack was sneaking around an enemy's position and was worried that the braying of his mules might give them away. One of his engineers, Clairborne Mason, had a solution. He tied all the mules' tails down, saying: "Mules never bray until they have their tails up." [22]

The confederate troops were often brutally short of supplies. They had little food, ragged clothes, few blankets to stave off the cold, and many men went barefoot. (An old lady once greeted them with tears in her eyes : "God bless your dirty, ragged souls!"[23] inspired more by their physical appearance than by their spiritual qualities.) But Jackson cared about his men, and they knew it. The men received their rations as promptly as possible; neither would he nor any of his staff officers be allowed to receive anything from the commissary until all the men were supplied first.

Jackson got called "Wagon Hunter" for his eagerness to capture Union supplies. General Taliaferro said, "Jackson was a wonderful gatherer of supplies. He had a pet commissary, General Banks." (Banks was a Union commander, and when his troops retreated they left their stores behind.)[24] Some people said Jackson was more eager to capture wagons with ammunition than with provisions, but that was only when he was advancing. As described by one of his officers, General Richard Taylor: "Without physical wants himself, he paid little heed to commissariat - but woe to the man who failed to bring up ammunition," and, "In advance, his trains were left far behind. In retreat, he would fight for a wheelbarrow."[25]

There was a streak of harshness, almost of cruelty in him too. Where others would yield, or compromise, he stood on his ground, even if it put him in a bad light. To him, the principle of the matter always came first, and usually, there was no second.

According to his first biographer R.J. Dabney, "His temper was recognized to be inflexible, without being petulant or aggressive." The first time this came up was at West Point. Another cadet substituted his dirty musket for Jackson's clean one. He possibly meant it as a joke, but Jackson did not see it that way. To him, it was a grave matter. Jackson demanded an investigation. He said he could identify his musket by a secret mark which he put on it. When the musket was found, and the culprit said it was just a mistake, Jackson asked for a court martial. Everyone else thought that Jackson was overreacting, but he kept insisting that it was a question of honor, that the other cadet had lied. It took a lot of persuading before Jackson backed down. Incidentally, the guilty cadet indeed had some character flaws. In his senior year at West Point, he was expelled, and in later years, he had an adventurous and not totally law-abiding career in the West, where he died.[26]

At the Virginia Military Academy, Major Jackson followed much the same inflexible course in his disputes with the students. In several cases, he demanded a court martial and dismissal of a student. This created such a dissatisfaction among students, and their parents as well, that a complaint about Jackson went to the Board of Visitors. The charge was that he was a terrible teacher, could not keep discipline in his classes and should be dismissed. When Jackson heard about it, almost a year later, he demanded a formal investigation of the charges. VMI's Superintendent, Colonel Smith, defended Jackson, and the Board was reluctant to dig into it, so both the original and Jackson's requests were tabled.

During the Civil War, Jackson's harsh righteousness often put him into conflict with his fellow officers. Some thought he was deliberately cruel. Such was the case with an officer in his command who asked for a short leave because his wife was ill. According to Jackson's aide, Kyd Douglas, the officer entreated Jackson with great emotion; "General, my wife is dying. I must see her!" A shade of sadness passed over the face of Jackson. But then immediately, he said in cold, merciless tones: "Man, man, do you love your wife more than your country?" and turned away. The wife died, and that officer never forgave Jackson.[27]

Stonewall Jackson was notorious for his harsh discipline. He had more men on report, or court martial, than any other Confederate officer. Once three of his raw, confused recruits deserted; when caught, they were court martialed and sentenced to be shot. Many thought it an unduly harsh punishment. A clergyman came to plead for them. He told the general: "Do you know you are sentencing these men's souls to hell." Jackson bodily threw the parson out of his tent, saying that he did not give him any advice on religious matters and asked none from him on military ones.[28] One of his fellow generals called him "the rudest and most arrogant pious man alive." But Jackson's view was, "When I receive orders, it is my habit to obey them, and when I give orders, I expect them to be obeyed." [29]

Even his friend Dabney Maury noted and regretted Jackson's intransigence, "He was at times cruelly unjust. His arrests of Hill, Winder and General Richard Garnett, three of the noblest officers in our service, were inexcusable."[30] But Jackson's guiding principle was: "Get rid of the unsuccessful man at once, and trust to Providence for finding a better."[31]

His feud with General A.P. Hill was perhaps worst. (This was the same Powell Hill with whom Jackson was at West Point and in Mexico.) Jackson accused Hill of lax discipline and took his command away from him. Hill was furious. He turned to Jackson and shouted: "If you take command of my troops in my presence, take my sword also," and gave it to him. "Consider yourself under arrest for neglect of duty," answered Jackson.[32] Afterwards, the two generals traded charges and counter charges, and General Robert E. Lee had to calm it down. The best he could do was to paper it over. Although Hill was present when Jackson was shot and behaved then with great compassion, he did not forgive and forget. He carried a grudge against Old Jack even after his death. Kyd Douglas, somewhat cattily commented that the difficulty between two such willful men was unavoidable, but "Hill never added one cubit to the high military reputation he had won under the leader he so cordially disliked."[33]

It was generally agreed that Jackson was ambitious. As a boy, he wanted to bring honor to his name. In early letters to his sister, Tom wrote, " ..my exertions would have to be great in order to acquire a fame. This course is most congenial to my taste. ." And in another one, "All the aid which will be desired will be in obtaining fame." And again, "I have some hopes that our ancient fame may be revived."[34] He both embraced this desire and fought against it.

General Dick Taylor said about him: "I saw an ambition as boundless as Cromwell's, and as merciless," and ". . .his ambition was vast, all-absorbing. He loathed it, perhaps feared it; but he could not escape it. . .it was his own flesh. He fought it with prayer."[35] And his good friend Dr. McGuire said of him: "Under the grave manner. . .were strong human passions dominated by his iron will - there was an intensely human ambition." His Civil War comrade in arms and biographer, Reverend Dabney, called it "thirst for distinction."

Upon his promotion to brigadier general, on June 17, 1861, Jackson wrote to Anna: "My promotion was beyond what I anticipated.... One of my greatest desires for advancement is the gratification it will give my darling, and the opportunity of serving my country more efficiently."[36] A few days before, on June 14, he chided Anna about suggesting he had gotten the promotion already, and that "the report owes its origin to Madam Rumor."[37] As it happened, the promotion was the result of lobbying in Richmond more than any specific military valor, but it was deserved nevertheless.

On October 7, 1861, less than four months after his promotion to brigadier general, Jackson was promoted again. He achieved his new rank, of major general, no doubt due to his leadership at First Manassas. About this, he wrote to Anna, "I am very thankful to that God who withholds no good thing from me for making me a major-general."[38] But not everyone was in favor of it. Some of the higher officers felt Jackson was getting beyond the point of his competence, and one of them expressed it: "I fear the Government is exchanging our best Brigade Commander for a second or third class Major General."[39]

It was shortly after this that Jackson tried to resign from the army. The Secretary of War, Judah P. Benjamin, whom Jackson did not particularly like, ordered him to recall troops from a mountain outpost to Winchester. Jackson was furious because he had other plans for them. He wrote to Richmond: "Your order requiring me to direct General Loring to return with his command to Winchester has been received and complied with." Then he added, "With such interference in my command, I cannot expect to be of much service in the field, and accordingly respectfully request to be ordered to report for duty to the Superintendent of the Virginia Military Institute. Should this application not be granted, I respectfully request that the President will accept my resignation from the Army." Emissaries from Richmond were sent, letters were written, and Jackson reconsidered, especially since he was promised the independent command he really wanted.[40]

Jackson was promoted once more, in October 1862, to lieutenant general. The Confederate Army was reorganizing with a new command structure, and Jackson was nominated by General Lee for one of the two new billets of lieutenant general. (The other one was General James Longstreet.) Lee's recommendation for the promotion read: "My opinion of General Jackson has been greatly enhanced during this expedition." Some military historians saw it as a rather guarded recommendation, as if Lee had some lingering doubts about Jackson's previous behavior.[41]

Whatever doubts Lee might have had, they were not about Jackson's bravery. In that same recommendation, Lee wrote: "He (Jackson) is true, honest and brave." Jackson's bravery sometimes bordered on recklessness. Soon after the first battle of Manassas, Jackson was asked: "How could you be so insensible to danger in a storm of shells and bullets as rained about your head when you hand was hit?" Jackson's reply was: "My religious belief teaches me to feel as safe in battle as in bed. God has fixed the time for my death. I do not concern myself about that."[42]

But perhaps this wasn't a complete answer. Jackson displayed much the same behavior as a young officer in Mexico, when his religious beliefs were still unformed. There too he exposed himself calmly and willfully to a hail of bullets. One cannon shot even went between his legs. At that time, he explained his behavior by saying he felt more alive, had a more perfect command of his faculties then at any other time. His brother-in-law Daniel Hill said; "I think that he loved danger for its own sake."[43]

To reach such an emotional peak, he may have been overdoing it sometimes. One day, during the Valley Campaign, he was riding with his aide Kyd Douglas, when he spotted bushes covered with blackberries. He immediately wanted to get some, but they just happened to grow very close to the enemy lines. Nevertheless, the two officers dismounted and went to pick them. Douglas acutely felt that there were as many bullets whizzing by as there were berries on the bushes, but the general seemed oblivious to it. But perhaps he was not, because suddenly, he paused and asked Douglas where he would prefer to be shot if he had to be shot somewhere. Pragmatic Douglas thought that getting shot just through his clothes would be best, but the general said that he had a definite prejudice against being shot in the back, and so he usually turned his face toward the firing.[44]

Jackson certainly was not completely oblivious to all danger; Daniel Hill, who knew him long and intimately, noted that Jackson had pre-battle "twitches." That when he started giving orders at the start of a battle his lips would often tremble, just like with other men, but he would not give in.[45] Jackson steadfastly believed, "Never take counsel of your fears."[46]

XIV.
JACKSON AND FAME

Northern mothers used to chasten their children saying, "Keep quiet or Jackson will get you." But some twenty years afterwards, a high ranking Union general wistfully confided to a former enemy, "I am sorry I never met Stonewall Jackson. He was easily the greatest military genius on either side of our late war."[1]

Jackson earned his fame because he won battles, but it was his personality that caught the public imagination. After his military exploits became known, the general started getting attention from the press (which he usually ignored), his many admirers, and even from young ladies. Newspapers in the South, North and even abroad published his biographies, often wildly inaccurate, and dwelled on his piety, military genius and his odd habits. Jackson's reaction to all this was unexpected: he enjoyed it, at least sometimes.

Jackson became a great favorite with the Southern ladies, who deluged him with gifts. Mrs. Graham, from Winchester, in whose house he stayed with Anna, sent two sponge cakes with invitation to come again. Other ladies kept sending delicacies, handkerchiefs, socks, gloves. There was the "beautiful summer hat from a lady from Cumberland" and a gift of handknit socks from one eighty year old Tennessee woman. In a letter to his wife, he asked her not to send him any more socks and kerchiefs as he had enough to last him for several years.[2]

One time, the general was approached by two young ladies who wanted a lock of his hair. The old Jackson would have dissolved in a sea of embarrassment, but this time, he agreed - provided they did not cut any gray hair. The ladies proclaimed that he had none, but Jackson disagreed: "Why, the soldiers call me Old Jack."[3] But another time, when he found himself in a circle of female admirers, he jokingly complained: "This is the first time I was ever surrounded by the enemy."[4] He had a point there, some young ladies got into a habit of stealing his uniform buttons as souvenirs, making the poor general look like a scarecrow.

On another occasion, two young girls stopped him on a street and started a conversation with him. Then suddenly, they leaned over and kissed him. Before the general could gather his wits and say something, the young ladies jumped into a carriage and drove away.[5] There was also the woman from Leesburg who ran out into the street, untied her scarf and threw it on the ground in front of the general on his horse. Jackson was surprised by it, but when an aide told him the woman wanted him to ride over the scarf, ". . he turned to her with a smile, took off his cap," and obliged her.[6]

With another young lady, his success was mixed. When he

was visiting her parent's home, she entertained him, playing the piano and singing. The general enjoyed it very much. As the impromptu concert was ending, Jackson expressed his appreciation and added: "Miss, won't you play a piece of music for me? They call it Dixie. I heard it the other day, and it was beautiful." There was a long silence. Then the young lady said: "But General, I just played it a few minutes ago."[7] Kyd Douglas who was there, later wrote that Jackson must have heard Dixie a thousand times before. Mrs. Jackson corroborated it. In her memoirs, she wrote how earlier, during her first visit to him, her husband made her sing Dixie again and again because he wanted to remember it, until she felt so ridiculous that she broke down in laughter.[8]

Not only women sent him gifts; Mr. Vilwig from Winchester sent him a comfortable armchair for use in his tent. Jackson was most appreciative and wrote to Anna: "I wish I could keep it until the close of the war, because my esposa would enjoy it."[9] He received a waterproof sleeping bag, several pairs of gauntlets, and from London came a box of flannel shirts, long woolen stockings, buckskin shirt, pair of boots, leather gloves, and "a very superior variegated colored blanket." Every post brought new articles. The general wrote Anna: ". .our ever-kind Heavenly Father gives me friends among strangers."[10]

But not all gifts were welcomed; one time, Jackson was presented with three havelocks - a covering to protect head and neck from sun. He commented on it to his wife, "I do not intend to wear them, I do not see the necessity in this climate ... the women would be better occupied by making haversacks for the soldiers."[11]

He received presents even from his comrades in arms. Given the state of Jackson's uniform, "faded, stained, frayed at the sleeves and missing buttons, and with patches that made him look a little like the Prodigal Son,"[12] General Jeb Stuart presented him with a spiffy brand new military jacket, complete with gold buttons and braid. When it was delivered by Stuart's staff assistant, Maj. von Borcke, Jackson viewed it uneasily and, folding the coat away, said: "Give Stuart my best thanks - the coat is much too handsome for me, but I shall take the best care of it and shall prize it highly as a souvenir." But the officer remarked that General Stuart would want to know if it fit, that General Jackson should try it on. It fit perfectly, so the officer suggested, as long as General Jackson was wearing it, why not keep it on for dinner. When Jackson emerged from his tent and walked to dinner, his fellow officers could not believe their eyes. The general's servant Jim almost dropped a platter with the turkey, and half of the men in the camp came running to stare and cheer.[13]

Once Jackson was visited by two British reporters, who were curious about this American Cromwell. They were warmly welcomed by Jackson. Before they could ask him any questions, he started talking about his fond memories of England, asking about the bishopric of Durham and cross examining his visitors about fine points of English history. They had no opportunity to question him on military matters.

After the interview ended, their American guide said: "Gentlemen, you have disclosed Jackson in a new character to me... You have made him exhibit finesse, for he did all the talking to keep you from asking too curious or embarrassing questions."[14] What he was referring to was not only that the general wanted to keep military secrets from the press, which he did, but also that he did not want to talk about his own accomplishments. He remained a modest man. As he once said: "Oh, if I have to blow my own horn, it will be a long time before it is blown."[15]

There were many people who would swear that Jackson did not have any sense of humor and that he never laughed. And there is much evidence to support it. Yet other people disagreed.

His former sister-in-law, Maggie Junkin Preston, thought that "his nature had a side that was decidedly sportive and rollicking." During Jackson's first marriage and afterwards, when they were living under the same roof, Jackson told her much about his childhood, West Point, Mexico. She remembered him as telling amusing stories and "getting so carried away with them, as almost roll from his chair in laughter."[16]

His VMI students were not sure. One day in class one cadet, well known as a jokester, solemnly asked him if a cannon could be so bent as to shoot around a corner. Jackson paused, gave the matter a thought, and then, without showing either irritation or a flicker of smile, he slowly replied: " Mr. Penn, I reckon hardly." The cadets could not decide if his gravity was real or assumed. The decision was, "If it was assumed, it was certainly well acted."[17]

His aide, Henry Kyd Douglas, said that Jackson "never told a joke, but rather liked to hear one now and then."[18] In Winchester in the winter of 1861, Jackson lived with a group of fellow officers, among them Colonel Preston from Lexington. After dinner, the officers used to talk and joke, while their general sat there, as Colonel Preston wrote his wife Maggie, ". . grave as a signpost, till something chances to overcome him, and then he breaks out into a laugh so awkward that it is manifest he had never laughed enough to learn how."[19]

But Jackson's good friend Dr. McGuire thought, ". . he often showed a keen sense of humor, when he laughed, he would catch one knee with both hands, lift it up, throw his body back, open wide his mouth, and his whole face and form be convulsed with mirth - but there was no sound." But, McGuire also said that amusing stories had to be "very plain ones" before Jackson would get them.[20]

The lighthearted General Jeb Stuart used to tease Jackson often and he did not seem to mind. But one time Jackson got even with Jeb. Stuart arrived in the middle of the night when Jackson was already asleep. It was a cold night, and Stuart was tired, so he went into Jackson's tent, where, taking off only his saber, he crawled into Jackson's bed and fell asleep. In the morning, Stuart got up first and was sitting by the fire when Jackson came out and addressed him, obviously mugging it: "General Stuart, I am always glad to see you. You might select better hours sometimes, but I am always glad to have you." Then rubbing his legs, he continued, "But, General, you must not get into my bed with your boots and spurs on and ride me around like a cavalry horse all night!"[21]

The friendship between the stodgy Jackson and effervescent Jeb Stuart puzzled many people. They called Stuart Prince Rupert and wondered how he could be a buddy of Cromwell (another popular nickname of Jackson). Although opposites, they got along enormously well. Stuart was deeply devoted to Jackson, and Jackson felt more comfortable with Jeb than with almost anyone else.

Even under the most trying conditions, Jackson did not swear and did not see any reason why anyone else should. There he was in agreement with R.E. Lee, Jeb Stuart and a few others, but certainly not with the majority of the Confederate army.

Jackson put down an otherwise good friend, Captain Imboden, by saying : "Nothing can justify profanity," when Imboden tried to apologize for having sworn furiously during a battle at First Manassas, because he thought he had been abandoned.[22] Jackson must have been even more tried by General Ewell and General Wise, who could not say a sentence without profanity. General Lee once upbraided Wise about it, but he replied: "General, you and Jackson can do all the praying for the Army of North Virginia, but for heaven's sake, let me do the cussing for one small brigade."[23]

But Jackson tolerated the cussing of his trusted quartermaster Major John Harman, a huge man who was a former stagecoach manager. Harman once managed to unsnarl a convoy stuck in fording a river, ". . .in a voice of stentor, he poured out a volume of oaths that would have excited the admiration of the most scientific mule-driver. The effect was electrical. The drivers were frightened and swore as best as they could, but far below the Major's standard. The mules caught the inspiration from a chorus of familiar words, and all at once made a break for the Maryland shore, and in five minutes, the ford was cleared." Jackson was there and heard it all. Harman came to apologize, saying that this was the only language mules would understand. But instead of a lecture, the general smiled and said, "Thank you, major..." This description is Major Imboden's.[24]

It was well known that Jackson did not drink and was opposed to drinking, especially by his men. The soldiers were getting liquor in packages from home or when they captured stores of the enemy, and it caused all sorts of problems with discipline. Soon after he took over his command in the Valley, the general gave an order that all wagons coming into the camp be searched and all spirits be confiscated.

This order may have had something to do with what happened a month earlier, in January of 1862, during the Romney expedition, which perhaps made Jackson sensitive to the issue of spirits. General Jackson and his men had been marching all day long in a cold sleety rain. Toward evening, his officers persuaded him to let the men stop and eat. The weather was miserable. Jackson, numb with cold, reached for his canteen and with a few deep gulps, drank a big portion of it, not even tasting what was going down. He probably thought it was some light wine, but a mistake was made, and he was drinking straight whisky. Soon afterwards, it had its effect: the general not only became warm, hot in fact, and started unbuttoning his coat and collar, but he also became talkative. To everyone's surprise he fell into a long and lively discourse. Those who were there said that he had never been so pleasant and amusing, before or later.[25]

During the second battle of Manassas, in late August 1862, his troops captured stores of the Union General Pope. Jackson's first order was to put the whisky storehouse under guard. When additional barrels of whisky, brandy and wine were "liberated" by his troops, he had them broken and the contents poured out, but the men, in desperation, fell on their faces and licked the liquor as it trickled on the ground.[26]

It is known that the general drank at least once more, but it was for a medicinal purpose. This happened in September 1862, during the Maryland campaign. Jackson's horse Little Sorrel had been stolen, and someone gave him a large gray mare, as big as a brewery horse. When he tried to mount her, she reared backward and threw him. He was stunned and bruised and lay there for a long time before moving, then an officer poured him a drink of brandy, and Jackson remarked: "I've always liked it. That's why I let it alone. I fear it more than Yankee bullets." But he drank it, though he stayed in his tent for the rest of the day. [27]

Kyd Douglas also remembered another occasion when the general actually mixed himself a "stiff toddy." He said that he liked the taste of it, and "I am the fondest man of liquor in this army. If I had indulged in my appetite, I would have been a drunkard."[28] But it is possible that Jackson's teetotalism embraced only hard liquor and not wine. When he was in New York City in the summer of 1858, he was shopping for wine for his sister and wrote her, "If I can't get Longworth's wine, will get Park's best Ohio wine,"[29] and Douglas suggests that in the Romney expedition, mentioned earlier, Jackson thought that his canteen contained wine, a present from an admirer from Winchester.[30]

XV.
HIS TIME HAD COME

Historians may debate whether or not the loss of Stonewall Jackson doomed the cause of the Confederacy, or shortened or prolonged the war. Whatever the military implications, there was something especially poignant about his death - he was a victim of "friendly fire."

It happened near Chancellorsville on May 2, 1863, just three days after Anna and baby Julia left. After a day of bloody and confusing skirmishes against the Union General (Fighting Joe) Hooker, Jackson and some of his officers rode out to check on the troops. They were riding through a wooded area full of brush and trees. Groups of soldiers from both armies were scattered through the woods. It was then about 8:30 in the evening and dusk. Suddenly shots rang out, and the general's mount, Little Sorrel, bolted and raced madly away. The general had been hit. General A.P. Hill was heard shouting: "Cease firing, cease firing," to no avail. The shots were being fired by the 18th North Carolina brigade, who believed they were firing on a group of Union officers.[1]

Jackson received one bullet through the palm of his right hand, another shattered his left arm at the elbow, and yet another hit the left hand and wrist. He was bleeding heavily. He remained conscious and even tried to stop the horse, but with little success. Soon Little Sorrel's reins were caught by a couple of officers from the Signal Corps. The general was placed on the ground, and General Hill gently took off his sword, belt and the bloody glove.[2]

There was the question if Jackson should be moved and risk additional hemorrhaging, or if a surgeon should be brought to treat him on the spot. Somebody said, "The enemy is within fifty feet and advancing." That decided it, but Jackson did not want to be carried, "If you can help me up, I can walk," he said.[3] Stumbling along between two of his companions, he did not want to be identified to the troops. They were to say he was just a wounded Confederate officer. He did not want any fuss because he feared his incapacitation would affect the troops' morale.

Eventually a litter came, and the general who was growing weaker was placed on it. Someone went to look for whisky to dull his pain. The woods were full of ricocheting shots. One of the litter bearers was shot in both hands, and his frightened buddy ran away. Jackson's three companions did not know what to do, they could not find replacement bearers. All the men they asked for help were afraid to leave the protection of the woods. In desperation, Captain Leigh told the Confederate soldiers the wounded man was Stonewall - and after that, they had more bearers than needed. Still, stumbling in the dark, one bearer tripped over some vines and fell. In the process, the litter tipped over with the general, who fell on the ground on his shattered arm. He was in severe pain, but not a sound came from him.[4]

Out of the woods, they found a waiting ambulance, and everyone felt relieved, except the general. The pain was becoming worse, and finally, he asked for some whisky - but there was no whisky anywhere. As the ambulance lurched over the bad roads they asked passing soldiers if they had any spirits - but none of them had any, or admitted to having any. The whisky and Dr. McGuire arrived at about the same time, both giving the general comfort. McGuire was an old friend who had treated him before, whom he trusted. "I hope you are not badly hurt, General," asked McGuire. "I am badly injured, Doctor; I fear I am dying," Jackson replied, "I am glad you have come."[5]

Although the general was in shock from pain and loss of blood, he did not die. Dr. McGuire was able to stop the bleeding by holding his hand to the artery, and the pain by giving the general more spirits and some morphia, as the ambulance continued on its way to the hospital at the Wilderness Old Tavern, some four miles away. They got there after 11 p.m. Later that night, Jackson's left arm was amputated about two inches below his shoulder. He was given anesthesia in the form of chloroform to dull the pain.

The surgical kit used by Dr. McGuire to amputate the general's arm can be seen at the Museum of the Confederacy in Richmond, Va. His arm also did not end on any anonymous pile of limbs which were found by most every military hospital of that time. Jackson's arm was buried in a fully marked grave in the Lacey family graveyard near Chancellorsville.

As Jackson was coming out of the anesthesia and drinking a cup of coffee, his close aide Sandie Pendleton arrived with a request from General Jeb Stuart. Stuart ended up in charge after Jackson's second in command, General A.P.Hill, was wounded. But Stuart, a cavalryman, had no experience leading infantry. He wanted to know what they should do next. At Pendleton's question, Jackson seemed to perk up. He started to respond, but suddenly stopped and said: "I don't know. Tell the general to do what he thinks best."[6] Later, after Pendleton left, he seemed lively enough. In an animated way, he discussed his surgery. He thought the chloroform was great; all he remembered was "a faint sound of delightful music, I believe it was the sawing of the bone. But I would not like to meet death under its influence, for that, one should have a clear mind."[7]

For the next day, Jackson continued to improve. General Lee wanted him moved to a safer place, away from the battlefront, so Jackson chose the home of Thomas Chandler, near Guinea Station about 25 miles away. Dr. McGuire, Chaplain Lacey and Captain Jimmy Smith, went along to take care of him.

With Smith, he carried on long religious-military discussions, at one point asking what guidance one would get from the Bible about writing military staff reports. Smith was doubtful that he could find something, but Jackson told him to look up "the narrative of Joshua's battle with the Amalekites; it has clearness, brevity, fairness, modesty; and it traces the victory to its right sources, the blessing of God."[8]

In the meantime, Anna's brother Joseph Morrison was sent to fetch her. General Lee, somewhat reassured about Jackson's condition, sent him a message: "Give him my affectionate regards, and tell him to make haste and get well, and come to me as soon as he can. He has lost his left arm; but I have lost my right arm."[9]

Except for a slight nausea, which Jackson treated with cold compresses on his stomach, he seemed to be healing well, until early Thursday, May 7. That night, he awoke nauseated. Dr. McGuire was asleep, the first sleep he had had, and Jackson did not want to wake him. He asked Jim Smith for another cold compress. But this time it did not help.

By dawn, Jackson was in such agony that he allowed Dr. McGuire to be awakened. When the doctor checked him, he found pneumonia. This, in the days before antibiotics, was a very dangerous disease, even more so for a man weakened by a wound. The doctor applied every available remedy - cupping, mercury, antimony, and opium, but there was no response.[10] McGuire wondered whether it could not have started when the general had fallen off the litter. Jackson himself thought it likely, he said the fall had been very hard and painful. But he kept reassuring Dr. McGuire not to worry, to leave the matter in the hands of God. Soon after this, drugged and weakened, he fell into a delirium.

About noon, Anna arrived. She had not been able to come sooner because the enemy cut the rail line. When she saw Thomas, she was appalled, "Oh, the fearful change since last I had seen him!...his fearful wounds, his mutilated arm, the scratches upon his face, and above all, the desperate pneumonia, which was flushing his cheeks, oppressing his breathing, and benumbing his senses."[11]

The next two days, Jackson drifted between consciousness and fevered sleep. Anna stayed at his side. He saw her worry and told her, "My darling, you must cheer up, and not wear a long face. I love cheerfulness and brightness in a sick-room," and later, "You are very much loved," and, "You are one of the most precious little wives in the world." But he did not want to see the baby, "Later, when I am feeling better,"[12] he said. He let Anna read to him from the Bible, and when he was most in pain, he asked her to sing him the spiritual songs they both loved. The song he especially wanted to hear was: "Show pity, Lord, O Lord forgive: Let repenting rebel live.."[13]

By Sunday morning, it was obvious that the end was near, and Thomas had to be told. Anna came to him and said that soon he shall be in heaven. Was he willing to go? "Yes, I prefer it, I prefer it," was his answer, "I had always wanted to die on Sunday."[14] For the last time, he saw baby Julia, who gave him a radiant smile. During his more lucid moments, he told Anna he wanted to be buried in Lexington and that she should return to her parents in North Carolina. As the day went on, his breathing

HIS TIME HAD COME

became more violent and then weaker. He drifted in and out of consciousness, talking, addressing his friends or family or issuing military orders. Finally, shortly after 3:00 p.m. on Sunday, May 10, 1863, General Stonewall Jackson stopped breathing. In the last moment, he said quite distinctly: "Let us cross over the river and rest under the shade of the trees."[15]

Stonewall Jackson Memorial Cemetery

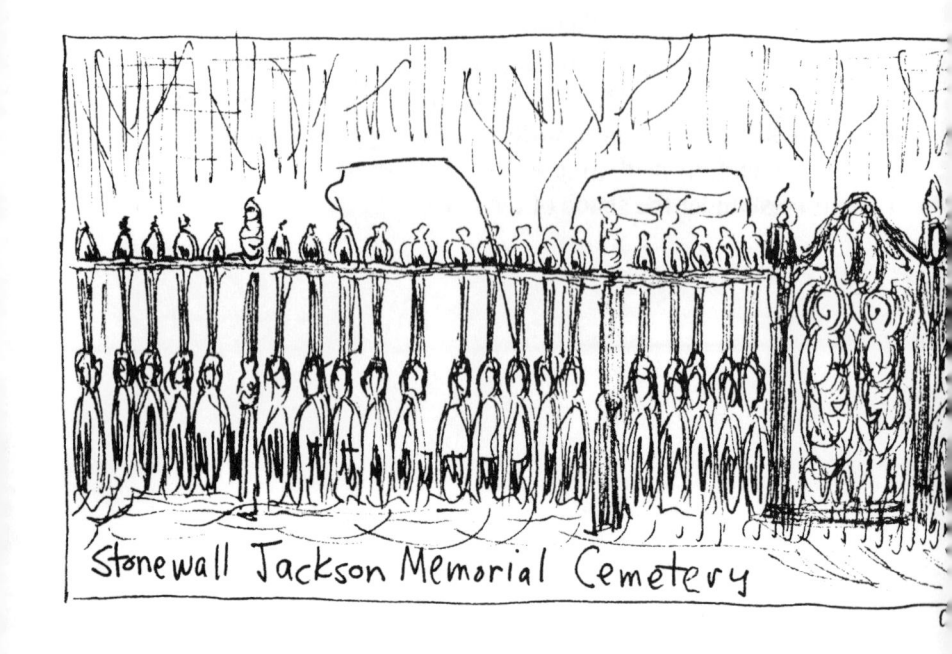

XVI.
RETURN TO LEXINGTON

It was Sandie Pendleton who was put in charge of Jackson's funeral. General Lee knew that Sandie came from Lexington and was especially close to Jackson, who treated him almost like a son.

Sandie had seen the general twice after he had been wounded, the first night shortly after his surgery when he came from the field with a message from General Jeb Stuart, and then not until the day Jackson died. By that time, Jackson was in semi-delirium, but he recognized Sandie and asked him, not about what was happening on the front, but because it was Sunday, who was preaching the sermon at the headquarters that day. When Sandie told him it was Mr. Lacey and that the entire army was praying for his recovery, Jackson said: "Thank God, they are very kind. It is the Lord's day; my wish is fulfilled. I have always wanted to die on Sunday." Sandie was so saddened by it that he went out to the porch and wept. As he saw Mrs. Jackson, he told her: "God knows, I would have died for him."[1] And he meant it.

Sandie Pendleton and Jimmy Smith dressed Jackson and placed him in a simple coffin, which was moved to the front hall of the Chandler office; there it stayed until its departure for Richmond. The next day, Monday, May 11, the funeral cortege left Guinea Station by a special train. It arrived in Richmond that afternoon. At all stations, people waited to say goodbye to Stonewall. Mrs. Jackson and the baby left the train early, to be spared the crowds, and were taken to the Governor's mansion by the governor's wife Mrs.Letcher.[2]

Thousands of Richmond citizens waited for them at the station. Sandie, Dr. McGuire, Jimmy Smith, Kyd Douglas and others accompanied the hearse to the Governor's Mansion in the Capitol Square, where it remained for the night. There, Jackson's body was embalmed and transferred to a metallic casket presented by the citizens of Fredericksburg.[3]

The following day, the body was moved to the Senate chambers to lay in state. The procession included every public official, military man, and plain citizen who could come. President Jefferson Davis, looking frail and ill, attended. Military units marched. Bands played funerary dirges. Bells were rung. The pallbearers were Jackson's staff members and generals of the army. Jim Lewis, the general's old servant, led Jackson's horse Little Sorrel. It was "very solemn and imposing because the mourning was sincere and heartfelt. There was no vain ostentation," wrote a contemporary diarist.

The final journey started on May 13th, when, after a brief service, the casket was taken back to the train, and on to Lynchburg. The train did not go as far as Lexington. In Lynchburg, the funeral party had to transfer to a packet boat, the

Marshall, which went up the James River and North River canals. Although it is less than fifty miles from Lynchburg to Lexington, it took from ten o'clock in the evening until the following afternoon, Thursday, May 14, to get there. In Lexington the corps of Virginia Military Institute cadets took the casket to VMI, where it was placed in Jackson's former classroom. In the funeral party were Governor Letcher, Senator G.A. Henry of Tennessee, and many representatives of the Confederate government as well as Dr. McGuire, Sandie Pendleton and Jim Smith. Also present were a company of veterans of the Stonewall Brigade, which happened to be in the county.

The funeral was, by request of Mrs. Jackson, the following day, May 15. There had been some confusion about the date, as the local newspaper announced it for the 16th. Jackson's casket was draped in the first Confederate flag ever made, which had been presented by President Davis to Mrs. Jackson. A simple service was conducted at the Lexington Presbyterian Church by Jackson's old pastor, Rev. Dr. White. He was assisted by Rev. Ramsey of Lynchburg and Rev. W.F. Junkin, Jackson's brother-in-law from his marriage to Ellie. Then the remains were taken two blocks up Main street to the cemetery, where the general was laid to rest.

"They will tell their children
Though all other memories fade
That they fought with Stonewall Jackson
In the old Stonewall brigade."[4]

WAR CASUALTIES

Stonewall Jackson was not the only Confederate general killed during the war. Of the 425 Confederate generals, 77 were killed or died as result of their wounds.

The total casualties for both sides were at least 618,000. The exact numbers are not known, but the Union side had between 2,500,000 to 2,750,000 men in the field, of whom 360,000 died. The Confederates lost 258,000 men, from 750,000 to perhaps 1,250,000 troops.

Yet it was not easy to kill a man, most of the casualties died from diseases. It was estimated that it took at least a man's weight in lead to kill him, or more. The Union army experts estimated that to kill one Rebel, they had to spend 240 lbs. of powder and 900 lbs. of lead.[5]

Casualties of Sharpsburg

EPILOGUE

After the funeral, Jackson's widow visited their house on Washington Street. She did not plan to live there, she was returning home to North Carolina to stay with her parents. On this sad occasion, a very detailed inventory of the house's furnishings was made. Anna shipped some of the furnishings to her new home, sold others and gave many things away as mementos. But she did not sell the house, she rented it out for the next forty plus years.

The rent from the house may have contributed to her support, as she was not a wealthy woman. Jackson's estate was a small one. After the war, when their slaves were freed, their investments in Confederate stocks and bonds were worthless, and even the tannery, where Jackson had a one third interest, was insolvent; there was little left. Anna Jackson was offered a hun-

EPILOGUE

dred dollars a month pension from the state of North Carolina, but she did not accept it. However, in 1890, she took a twenty dollars a month pension from the United States government to which she was entitled as a widow of a Mexican War veteran.

Anna Jackson never remarried, not because she lacked suitors, but because she was too devoted to the memory of her husband. In her memoirs, she said: "I just could not give up the name." She was not considered to be any great beauty, but was loved for her character and sweet temperament. A colleague of her husband described her (on the occasion of her visit during the war to her husband) as "slightly built and tolerably good looking." She lived until her eighty-fourth year and was admired by both Southerners and Northerners. She wrote her memoirs about her husband in part to refute some of the more bizarre and sensationalistic books and articles which were being published about him.

Jackson's daughter Julia grew up, eventually marrying William E. Christian, a Richmond newspaperman, with whom she had two children - a daughter, born in 1887, named Julia Laura and in 1888, a son, Thomas Jonathan Jackson. Julia Jackson Christian died a year later of typhoid, at the age of twenty-seven. After the death of their mother, the children were raised by an aunt, Susan Christian, and by their grandmother Jackson who, in later years, lived with her granddaughter Julia. Anna died on March 24, 1915, in Charlotte, North Carolina.

CHRONOLOGY OF JACKSON'S LIFE

1824	January 20 or 21, born in Clarksburg, (West) Virginia.
1826	March 26, his father Jonathan Jackson dies.
1830	His mother, Julia Neale Jackson, marries Blake B. Woodson, and moves to present Fayette County, (W.) Virginia. Thomas goes to his stepgrandmother, Mrs. Edward Jackson, near Weston, (W.) Virginia.
1831	His mother dies.
1841	Teaches school, later is appointed constable of Lewis County, (W.) Virginia.
1842	Receives appointment to West Point.
1846	July 1, graduates from West Point. Leaves for Mexico in August. Arrives in Monterey in November.
1847	Battles of Vera Cruz in May, Contreras and Cherubusco in August. Jackson advances in rank to first lieutenant, then brevet rank of captain in August and brevet rank of major in September.
1848	June - returns to United States and is stationed at Fort Hamilton, N.Y.
1849	April - is baptised in Episcopalian church.
1850	October - arrives in Florida. In December, comes to Fort Meade.
1851	February - applies for leave or transfer. May - leaves Florida. Reports at Virginia Military Institute August 13. On November 22, joins Lexington Presbyterian Church.
1852	Resigns from U.S. Army, February 22; approved February 29. On May 6, Cadet J.A. Walker court martialed

CHRONOLOGY OF JACKSON'S LIFE

on Jackson's charges. July - Jackson visits Rockbridge Alum Springs. November - joins Bible Society.

1853 March - joins Franklin Society. August 4, marries Elinor Junkin.

1854 January - elected director of bank, applies for a position at University of Virginia. July - with Ellie visits sister Laura. October - Elinor and baby die.

1855 July - Jackson visits sister Laura in Beverly.

1856 July - September - Jackson tours Europe. He visits: Glasgow, Stirling Castle, Edinburgh, York, London, Antwerp, Brussels, Waterloo, Aix La Chappell, Bonn, Frankfort, Heidelberg, Baden Baden, Strasbourg, Basle, Lucern, Brience, Thurn, Geneva, Mer de Glas, Alps by the Simplon Pass, Milan, Venice, Mantua, Modena, Florence, Pisa, Leghorn, Naples, Vesuvius and Rome.

1857 July 16 - marries Mary Anna Morrison.

1858 Daughter Mary Graham born in May, dies on 25th.

1859 January 19 - moves into house on Washington Street in Lexington. Nephew Thomas Arnold visits.

December - Jackson takes VMI cadets to Harper's Ferry for the execution of John Brown.

1860 July - August - visits hydropathic establishment at Brattleboro, Vermont.

1861 April - leaves Lexington with VMI cadets at start of Civil War. Appointed colonel, assumes command at Harper's Ferry.
June - commissioned brigadier general.
July - battle of First Manassas.
September - wife Mary Anna visits him.

October - gets command of Shenandoah Valley.

1862 January - Winchester. Mary Anna visits him. Romney campaign. Tries to resign.
March - battle of Kernstown, where he is defeated.
May - beginning of the Shenandoah campaign. Victorious at McDowell, Front Royal, Winchester.
June - battles of Cross Keys, Port Republic. Seven Days Campaign before Richmond begins on 25th, where Jackson is less than successful.
August 9 - Jackson returns to Shenandoah Valley, defeats Banks at Cedar Mountain. With Lee, defeats Pope at Second Manassas.
September - captures Harper's Ferry. Battle of Antietam, the bloodiest single day of the war.
October - is placed in command of Second Corps, becomes lieutenant general.
November - daughter Julia is born.
December - establishes winter quarters at Moss Neck.

1863 April - wife and baby daughter visit him.
May - battle of Chancellorsville, Jackson is wounded and dies on May 10.

PEOPLE AND EVENTS

Laura Jackson Arnold (b.1826 - d.1911) was Jackson's sister. In 1844, she married Jonathan Arnold (1802-1883) of Beverly, she was his third wife. They had four children, three of whom survived to maturity: Thomas Jackson, Anna Grace and Stark William. Beverly was in Union hands throughout the war, and Laura became a Union sympathizer. She occupied herself with nursing Union soldiers. There was a rumor that she became involved romantically with one or more of them. In 1870, her husband divorced her. She became estranged from her family and children, and, as some said, bitter and irrational. Till her death at eighty, she refused to call her brother Stonewall. In 1877, Anna Jackson wrote about her: "She must be an unhappy woman, cut off as she is from part of her family. Mr. Arnold so set against her, but she still wants to see his house, which is a great annoyance to him and to Tom." But perhaps Laura was maligned, and it was Mr. Arnold who was the more difficult spouse. In October 1859, in a letter to Laura, Jackson mentions he would have written two weeks ago, "but feared Mr. Arnold (her husband) would get suspicious of frequent letters."

Thomas Jackson Arnold (1845-1933), Laura Arnold's eldest son. Stonewall Jackson was especially close to Tom and treated him like a son. Tom Arnold became a lawyer and collector for the port of San Diego in California. In 1876, he married Mary Eugenia Hill, daughter of Daniel Harvey Hill and Isabella Hill Morrison (Anna Jackson's sister). Tom Arnold greatly admired his famous uncle and wrote a book about him called *Early Life and Letters of General Thomas J. Jackson*. This is an excellent book, except that the author often edited these letters and excised anything which showed Jackson or any member of the family in a less than adulatory vein.

Bernard E. Bee (1824-1861) was a six foot tall North Carolinian. He was a 1845 graduate of West Point, where he knew Jackson. General Bee is credited with giving Jackson the nickname Stonewall. It happened during the first battle of Manassas when Bee was supposed to have said that Jackson was standing there like a stone wall while other units were retreating. Some fellow officers suggested that Bee meant it not as a compliment but that Jackson was blocking his advance. That was the theory of Col. J.C. Haskell. However, most historians deny this interpretation. Prior to this fateful encounter with Jackson at Manassas, they fought together in Mexico and were together at Harper's Ferry in the early months of the Civil War.

The Brake relatives As a child, Tom Jackson was sent to live with his Brake relatives, but he was not happy there and ran away. The Brake connection was through Tom's grandfather Edward Jackson, whose first wife Mary Hadden had six children - Tom's father Jonathan among them. Two of their daughters married Brakes; Rachel married Jacob Brake (b.1875), and Mary Hadden married Isaac Brake (b.1797). Edward's second wife was Elizabeth Brake (b.1772) and was probably related to Isaac and Jacob. It is generally believed that Tom stayed with Isaac.

Julia Laura Jackson Christian (1887-1991) was born Anna but renamed Julia after the death of her mother. She was Stonewall Jackson's only granddaughter. In 1907, she married Edmund Randolph Preston (1880-1957) with whom she had six children. She lived to her 104th year, dying in September 1991. Her husband died in 1957. Edmund Preston was the grandson of Stonewall's VMI colleague, J.T.L.Preston, and Maggie Junkin Preston was his step-grandmother.

Thomas Jonathan Jackson Christian (1888-1952) Stonewall's only grandson, graduated from West Point in 1911, and served in both World Wars, retiring with the rank of colonel. He was married three times, and had five children. His first son, Thomas Jonathan Jackson (b. 1917) graduated from West Point in 1939 and was shot down over France in 1944 and killed. His youngest son was born in 1952 and also named Thomas Jonathan Jackson.

William Christian (Willie), (1856-1936) husband of Stonewall's only child Julia, came from a Richmond banking family. He was a graduate of the University of Virginia. After graduation, he spent a year touring Europe and then worked in his grandfather's bank. He did newspaper work in California, where both of his and Julia's children were born, and where Mary Anna Jackson accompanied them. In later years, he was the editor of the Charlotte, *N.C. Democrat.*

Rev. Robert Lewis Dabney (1820-1898) A native Virginian, Dabney joined the Confederate forces as a chaplain. However, in early April 1862, he accepted the post of chief of staff for Jackson. This surprised and even alarmed Jackson's military command, as Dabney had no military training and hardly any military experience. One of them commented on it, saying: "I concluded that Old Jack must be a fatalist when he put an Ironside Presbyterian parson as his chief of staff." Their opinion was confirmed when they saw Dabney in person. He came to his post dressed in clergyman's black frock coat, beaver hat and, even on horseback, carried an umbrella. Of course, the men made fun of him. When Jackson found out about it, he invited Dabney and the rest of the staff for a ride, leading them all at a gallop through thick woods. In the course of this, Dabney's umbrella was torn and his beaver hat lost. The next day, he appeared in borrowed uniform, which he wore until he left Jackson's staff three months later. It was said that he was a conscientious officer but more effective in camp than in the field. He returned to a religious life and wrote Jackson's biography, which was published for the first time towards the end of the Civil War. Dabney was a die hard Southerner and found it difficult to reconcile himself to the defeat of the Confederacy. In his book, *Life and Campaigns of Lieut.-Gen. Thomas J. Jackson,* he was unabashedly partisan, and not always accurate. General Robert E. Lee had to correct some of his statements.

Henry Kyd Douglas (1840-1903) was born in Shepherdstown, now West Virginia, but shortly afterward, his family moved to the other side of the Potomac, which was in Maryland. He graduated from Franklin and Marshall College in Lancaster, Pennsylvania and then studied law at the school of Judge Brockenbrough in Lexington, while Jackson lived there; however if they met, there is no record of it. In 1860, Douglas was admitted to the bar. He became the youngest member of Jackson's staff and later served under several other Confederate generals. Douglas was wounded six times and captured once and imprisoned for eight months. Paroled in March 1864, he finished the war a commander of the Light Brigade. His troops fired the last shot at Appomattox, and were allowed to be the last brigade to surrender. After the war, he became a lawyer in Hagerstown, Maryland. He never married. His book, *I Rode with Stonewall*, was put together at the end of the century from notes and journals and an earlier book that he wrote during and immediately after the war, but did not publish. He signed himself usually as H.Kyd Douglas so there is an implication he did not use his first name. This is why I have referred to him as Kyd Douglas in this book.

Richard Stoddert Ewell (1817-1872) graduated from West Point in 1840. During the Civil War, General Ewell fought under Jackson, and after Jackson's death, took over his command. However, he was unprepared for the loose style of command practiced by Lee, and perhaps affected by the loss of a leg at the beginning of the second Manassas. In any case, Ewell could not fill Jackson's shoes. To his troops, he was known as "Old Baldy." After the war, he retired to a farm in Tennessee.

William H. French Jackson's commanding officer in Florida, where Jackson clashed with him over both military and personal matters, joined the Union army during the Civil War. Generals French and Jackson fought against each other in September 1862 at Sharpsburg, Md., although Jackson may not have been aware of it.

Ambrose Powell Hill (1825-1865) General A. P. Hill, was born in Culpeper County, Virginia on November 9, 1825. He entered West Point with Jackson, but during his second year leave, he caught gonorrhea and missed several months of school. His life-long ill health may have been related to this episode. He graduated from West Point in 1847, 15th in a class of 38, later serving in the Mexican War and in the Seminole Wars, staying in the U.S. army until 1861, when he joined the Confederate army. In the last days of the Civil War, on April 2, 1865, General Hill was shot at Petersburg, Virginia - the bullet severing his thumb and gauntlet, then piercing his heart. Despite his feud with Jackson, Hill was highly regarded by General Lee and loved and admired by his men. In private life, he was genial and approachable. However, his ill health often incapacitated him and may have caused some of the defeats he suffered in the field.

Daniel Harvey Hill (1821-1889) was born in South Carolina. He was Jackson's brother-in-law, married to Anna's sister Isabella. Hill graduated from West Point three years before Jackson (28th in a class of 56), but did not meet him until Mexico. Hill resigned from the army in 1849, taught mathematics at Washington College and Davidson College and, at the start of the Civil War, was the superintendent of North Carolina Military Institute. General Hill tended to be rather outspoken, and his habit of disagreeing with his commanding officers affected his military career. A sample of his official prose on an application for transfer from infantry to the band reads: "Respectfully forwarded, disapproved. Shooters are more needed than tooters." After the war, Hill became a newspaper and magazine editor and later returned to an academic career as a college president at the University of Arkansas and then from 1885-89, at Georgia Military Academy. Hill's effect on Jackson's life was great: through him, Jackson came to VMI, he introduced him to both of his wives, and he was instrumental in Jackson joining the Presbyterian church.

Isabella Sophia Morrison Hill (1825-1904) was an older sister of Anna Jackson and the wife of Daniel Hill, with whom she had ten children (four died in childhood). Their second child

Mary Eugenia (1852-1934) married Jackson's nephew Thomas Arnold. Isabella, like her sisters, was a graduate of Salem College.

John Daniel Imboden (1823-1895) was born in Virginia. He graduated from Washington College and was a lawyer and legislator. He organized the Staunton Artillery. During the Civil War, he fought in many battles, including Piedmont and New Market, later he was felled by typhoid and was sent to Aiken, S.C. on prison duty. He became a Brigadier General in October 1862. After the war, he was a lawyer and land developer, and wrote articles about the war and about Virginia's natural resources. He was married five times.

Jackson Family The first Jackson in America was John Jackson (1715-1801), born in Coleraine, Londonderry, Ireland. He emigrated to Maryland in 1748, and in 1758 moved to Virginia. He was a member of the County Court, a lieutenant in the militia in 1787, and during the Revolutionary War, he fought in the Battle of King's Mountain. He was supposed to have been a rather short and spare man, but courageous and of sound judgment. In 1755, John married Elizabeth Cummins (1733?-1828), they had seven children, including George who became a member of the Virginia Assembly and the Virginia Constitutional Convention, and Edward Jackson, Tom's grandfather. Elizabeth Cummins was born in London. She was raised by a maiden aunt who left her one thousand pounds of sterling. With her inheritance, Elizabeth emigrated to America where she met and married John Jackson. She was remembered as a strong and rather tall woman, brave and resourceful. She fought off Indian attacks and even bought in her own name 3,000 acres of land. Tom's grandfather Edward Jackson (1759-1828) was married twice; with his first wife Mary Hadden (1764-1796), he had six children: George, David, Jonathan (who was Tom's father), Rachel (who married Jacob Brake), Mary Hadden, (who married Isaac Brake), and Rebecca. In 1799, Edward married his second wife Elizabeth Brake (1772-1835), and they had nine children born between 1800 and 1821.

PEOPLE AND EVENTS

Cummins was the second eldest one and the eldest son.

Cummins Jackson (1802-1849) was Tom's uncle on his father's side. Tom lived with him from age five until he went to West Point at the age of eighteen. He was often thought to be a bad moral influence on Tom (see note in Ch I.). Cummins never married; he died in 1849 in Shasta County, California, where he had gone during the Gold Rush. Cummins was a reasonably wealthy man, having inherited the Jackson Mill and land, but he died intestate. The property had to be divided among about a hundred relatives, so Tom's share of it was just a couple of hundred dollars, which he gave to another relative who had taken care of him while he was a child. Thomas Jackson visited Jackson Mill for the last time in the summer of 1852, with his cousin Sylvanus White, and found only Negroes living there.

Jonathan Jackson Tom's father, was born 1790, the third son of Edward Jackson and Mary Hadden. He was educated in academies in Clarksburg and Parkersburg. By 1810, he was admitted to the bar in Harrison County after studies at the law offices of his cousin, John G. Jackson of Clarksburg. Later, he was appointed Commissioner of Internal Revenue, and his father gave him some properties. However, he mismanaged his accounts to the tune of $3,500 and was removed from the office. In 1818, he married Julia Beckwith Neale of Parkersburg, and they settled in a small house on Main Street in Clarksburg. Jonathan died on March 26, 1826 of typhoid fever contracted from nursing his eldest child, Elizabeth. (Elizabeth died on March 5.) After his death, it was found that he died broke. It was generally said that he had signed notes for too many of his friends, gambled, and in general mismanaged his finances. His brothers from the Masonic Fraternity came to the rescue of his widow by finding her a small one-room cottage to live in.

Julia Beckwith Neale Jackson (Woodson) (1798-1831) was Tom's mother. She was actually named Judith, but was always known as Julia. Her parents Thomas Neale and Margaret Winn Neale came from old Eastern Virginia families. The original

Neales, known then as either O'Neal or O'Neill, came from Limerick County in Ireland some time between 1640 and 1660. Julia was attractive, quick-witted, lively and well educated. She was described as having dark brown hair and dark gray eyes. She married Jackson at the age of 19, he was 28. After the death of Tom's father in 1826, she tried to earn her living by running a school. In 1830, she married for a second time to another lawyer, fifteen years older than she. Blake Woodson (1783-1833) was a widower with eight children, but none of them lived at home. Julia died about a year later, a few months after bearing her fifth child, a son, William Wirt Woodson (1831-1875). Blake Woodson remarried about a year after Julia's death and died a few months later.

Jackson's house on Washington Street in Lexington went through some good times and some bad times. During the Civil War, Lexington was occupied by the Union forces, but other than at the VMI campus, the town did not suffer a great deal of damage. But time took its toll. After many years as rental property, the house deteriorated so badly that some of the town's citizens wanted to buy it from Mrs. Jackson, tear it down, sell the bricks as souvenirs, and from the proceeds, build on the site a monument to Stonewall Jackson. Instead, shortly after the turn of the century, the local chapter of United Daughters of the Confederacy persuaded Mrs. Jackson to sell them the house so that they could make it into the first hospital in Rockbridge County. As it happened, the ladies made this decision without having any funds for it, but through various fund raising activities, managed to get a subscription of $2,000, enough for the purchase. Mrs. Jackson was pleased with this plan; she did not want the house turned into a shrine, but she thought her husband would have approved of something as useful as a hospital. It was named Stonewall Jackson Hospital, and it remained as such until the 1950s when a new Stonewall Jackson Hospital was built. In the late 1970s, the house was restored to what it had been in Jackson's day and opened to the public as a museum.

Jackson siblings Jonathan and Julia Neale Jackson had four children. Elizabeth (1819-1826), Warren (1821-1841), Thomas (1824-1863) and Laura (1826-1911, see Laura Arnold). Elizabeth died of typhoid in 1826. Her father had nursed her, became infected and within a week died of it too. The next day, Laura was born. Warren died of tuberculosis at twenty, perhaps as a result of malaria, which he had caught during his and Tom's adventure on the Mississippi River.

Rev. Dr. George Junkin (1790-1868) was father of Stonewall's first wife Elinor (Ellie) Junkin. He was a native of Pennsylvania, graduate of Theological Seminary in New York, and served as president of three colleges; Lafayette College, Pa., Miami University, Ohio and Washington College, Lexington, Va. He and his wife Julia Rush Miller (1795-1854) had nine children. Margaret (Maggie) was the eldest one. Dr. Junkin was a Union sympathizer and in 1861, at the start of the war, he resigned from Washington College, where he had served since 1848, and returned to Pennsylvania. It has been said that when he reached Pennsylvania, he got out of his carriage and cleaned off Southern soil from the carriage wheels and from the horses hooves. His daughter Maggie, a writer and a poet married to J.T.L. Preston, was a Southern sympathizer, but after the war, the family renewed ties as if nothing had happened.

Rev. Beverly Tucker Lacey was known for his original and powerful sermons. Jackson appointed him to be an unofficial chaplain of his 2nd Corps. It was Lacey who arranged for Jackson's amputated arm to be buried in the family cemetery located nearby at Elwood. It was then on a plantation owned by his brother, Maj. J. Horace Lacey. Today it belongs to the National Park Service.

Robert Edward Lee (1807-1870) General Lee was the son of Revolutionary War hero "Light Horse" Harry Lee (who however in later years fell into disrepute). He attended West Point, graduating in 1829, second in his class, with not a single demerit on his record. He was posted to the engineers and served in many posts across the land. In 1852, he was appointed a superintendent of West Point. Although Jackson and Lee both served in the Mexican War, there is no record that they met there. Jackson most likely knew about Lee but possibly not vice versa. Their first known contact was in 1854, when Lee wrote a letter recommending Jackson for a position of a mathematics professor at the University of Virginia. However, there is no evidence that Lee knew Jackson personally, the letter was written in his role of Superintendent of the U.S. Military Academy at West Point. Their military collaboration began during the Valley Campaign. After the April 9, 1865 surrender at Appomattox, Lee found himself reunited with his family but without a home for them. Lee was married to Mary Ann Randolph Custis, great-granddaughter of Martha Washington, with whom he had seven children. The family home, Arlington, was now a Federal cemetery. Lee did not want to take advantage of his former position in earning his living, and he also wanted to put the war behind him in a positive way. In this spirit, to everyone's surprise, he accepted the offer to become president of Washington College. The college was located in Lexington, Virginia, Jackson's old home. Lee's starting salary there was $1,500. None of the Lee family had ever been in Lexington, but they knew of the college because Lee's father had persuaded George Washington to make a generous gift of canal stock to the school, then known as Liberty Hall. The renaming to Washington College followed. R.E. Lee served as the school's president until his death in 1870, at the age of sixty-three. In his honor, the school was later renamed Washington & Lee University.

Jim Lewis Stonewall Jackson's servant was, according to Henry Kyd Douglas, "a handsome mulatto, in the prime of life, well-made and with excellent manners, but perhaps altogether true only to the general." Jim admired Jackson's temperance views but not for himself - he was supposed to have been fond both of liquor and a quiet game of cards. According to Douglas, "When the general died, Jim's grief was almost inconsolable. He then attached himself to Sandie Pendleton, but when he fell also, Jim seemed to break down. He grew sad and went home on a short furlough. But he was taken ill and died in Lexington."

Little Sorrel After Jackson fell, the horse ran away but was found and returned by a Confederate soldier. Later, the horse was sent to the Morrison farm in North Carolina and finally came to Mrs. Jackson, but it is doubtful she ever rode him. His original name was Fancy. Mrs. Jackson said that after the war, renamed Old Fancy, he became the family favorite, especially her father's. He was used as both a riding and carriage horse. Mrs. Jackson wrote that he was a clever horse who knew how to open latches and gates with his mouth. He would let himself out of the stable, go to the pasture and let out all the horses and mules and lead them, like a general, to the grain fields. Fences did not faze him, as he could lift off the rails with his mouth until they were low enough to jump over. Old Fancy lived to the age of thirty, and after his death in 1886 at the Soldier's Home in Richmond, Va., his hide was mounted and is on view in the VMI museum. His bones are not mounted, they are stored in the VMI biology department.

John Bankhead Magruder (1807-1871) entered West Point in 1826, one year after R.E.Lee, graduating in 1830. He served in the Seminole and Mexican wars and was noted for his bravery but also for always seeking the spotlight. He was known as a dandy and for his lavish entertainments. "Prince John" and "El Capitan Colorado" were some of his nicknames. However, he tended to be imperious and ill tempered. During the Civil War, for a short while, he served under Jackson. In the Seven Days Battle at Malvern Hill, General Magruder mistakenly led his division in the wrong direction, contributing to the Confederate defeat. He spent the rest of the war fighting in Texas. After the war, he was one of the few generals who refused to ask for a parole and instead went back to Mexico, where he offered his services to Emperor Maxmilian. After Maxmilian's death in 1867, Magruder returned to the United States and lectured about his adventures. There seems to be some doubt about Magruder's birth date, as it is listed as 1807, or 1810. He died in relative poverty.

Dabney H. Maury (1822-1900) was a nephew of Matthew Fontaine Maury, the founder of the science of oceanography, who was like a father to him (Dabney's father died early). Dabney graduated from the University of Virginia and studied law before entering West Point. He graduated from West Point the same year as Jackson, in 1846, 37th in a class of 59. After his service in Mexico, he became an instructor at West Point, and later served on the frontier. Maury was promoted to Brigadier General and later Major General in the Confederate Army, serving mostly with the Army of the West on the Gulf. After the Civil War, penniless, he returned to Virginia and established a school in his home town of Fredericksburg. He also organized the Southern Historical Society. Later, he went to New Orleans where he was in various businesses and then was appointed an ambassador to Colombia. He wrote a breezy, gossipy book of memoirs called *Recollections of a Virginian* which was published in 1894.

Dr. Hunter Holmes McGuire (1835-1900) was born in Winchester, Virginia. He was educated at the University of Pennsylvania and the Jefferson Medical College. During the Civil War, he became medical director of the Army of the Valley and Jackson's physician. He was described by a contemporary as "blunt, good humor and full of honest life." After the war, he founded the University College of Medicine in Richmond and served as the president of the American Medical Association.

Morrison family Mary Anna Morrison, Jackson's wife was one of ten surviving children of the Rev. Dr. Robert Hall Morrison (1798-1889) and his wife Mary Graham (1801-1864), daughter of General Joseph Graham. Rev. Morrison was a Presbyterian minister and the founder of Davidson College in North Carolina. At the time of Anna's marriage to Jackson, her family lived in Lincoln County, North Carolina. Anna's mother died shortly after the end of the war. Her father lived to the age of ninety

PEOPLE AND EVENTS

years.

Morrison siblings The children of Rev. Robert Morrison and Mary Graham Morrison were:

Isabella Sophia (1825-1904) graduate of Salem College, she married Daniel Harvey Hill in 1848.

William Wilberforce (1826-1865) educated at Washington College, later he was private secretary to his uncle, Governor William Graham.

Harriet Abigail (1828-1897) graduate of Salem College, she was a writer, publishing articles in many magazines; in 1849, she married James Patton Irwin. At her home, Jackson's only surviving child was born.

Mary Anna (1831-1915) graduate of Salem College, she married Thomas Jonathan Jackson in 1857.

Eugenia Erixene (1833-1858), she was the family beauty, but died suddenly of typhoid fever. She married, in 1854, Rufus Barringer, a lawyer from Concord, N.C., who later became a Confederate general.

Sarah M. (1834-1838)

Elizabeth Lee Davidson (1837-1838)

Susan Washington (1838-1886) married in 1861 to Alphonso Calhoun Avery. Susan was known in her family for her musical talent; she received voice training at the Edgewood Seminary in Greensboro, N.C., and at the Peace Institute in Raleigh. Her husband served as a Confederate colonel and later as North Carolina Supreme Court justice.

Laura Panthea (1840-1920) was also an author and a leader in religious and civic organizations. She married, in 1869, John Edmunds Brown, a lawyer who served in the Confederate Army as a colonel and was wounded on his head.

Joseph Graham (1842-1906) attended VMI, later was on

Jackson's staff, helped to carry him from the battlefield when he was wounded and was with him at the time of his death. Afterwards, Joseph was wounded four times and in 1864, lost half of his foot (all but the heel) in a battle. After the war, he became a pioneer in cotton manufacturing in North Carolina. In 1872, he married Jane Elizabeth Davis.

Robert Hall, Jr. (1843-1922) At the age of sixteen Robert was made aide to General D. H. Hill (his brother-in-law). He was captured in a battle and imprisoned. After the war, he finished his studies at Davidson College and studied medicine. In 1882, he married Lucy Andrews Reid.

Alfred James (1849-1876) graduated from Davidson College, became a lawyer and served in the North Carolina State Legislature. Later, he studied for the ministry but died unexpectedly while travelling home. In 1876, he married Portia Lee Atkinson.

Alexander Swift (Sandie) Pendleton was the only son of Rev., later Brig. General, W.N. Pendleton, rector of the Episcopal church in Lexington, Virginia. In 1863, Sandie married his sweetheart Kate Corbin (of the Corbin family where Jackson spent the winter of 1862-63 and where he played with little Jane Corbin.) Sandie was shot through his abdomen and after five days, died on September 23, 1864, just five days before his twenty-fourth birthday.

Rev. William N. Pendleton (1809-1883), was an 1830 graduate of West Point. Before the war, he was the rector of Episcopal Church in Lexington. During the war, he commanded the Rockbridge Artillery battery, which consisted of mostly Lexington men. Among them were a son of General Lee, seven Masters of Art from the University of Virginia and forty-two other college graduates, as well as nineteen theological students, most serving as privates. (They named their four guns "Matthew," "Mark," "Luke," and "John," and Pendleton is supposed to have given orders to fire as: "May the Lord have mercy on their poor souls - Fire!") General Pendleton, impoverished by the war, returned to Lexington to his old church, where he became the Lee family's pastor.

Margaret (Maggie) Junkin Preston (1820-1897) was an older sister of Jackson's first wife Ellie. After her father Rev. Dr. Junkin resigned as president of Washington College in 1861 and returned to Pennsylvania, Maggie stayed in Lexington as the wife of J.T.L. Preston (1811-1892). Her husband survived the war and returned to his post as a classics teacher at VMI. In addition to her seven step-children, Maggie had two sons of her own. Maggie was seen by her social circle as a literary lioness, although her poetic and literary talents were more modest. Maggie never attended any school, yet she was knowledgeable on almost any topic. She gave up her writing for ten years after her marriage to Preston, because as she said, he did not consider it a suitable occupation for his wife, but she kept a private journal, which along with her correspondence, her step-daughter, Elizabeth Preston Allan, later arranged into a book. There is no doubt that Maggie adored Jackson, whether it was a sisterly feeling or something more is difficult to tell. In later years, she was hard of hearing and had to use an ear trumpet. Her husband died in 1892 and shortly afterwards, Maggie suffered a minor stroke and spent the rest of her life in a wheelchair. She died at the age of seventy-six in Baltimore at the home of her son Dr. George Preston.

James Ewell Brown (Jeb) Stuart (1833-1864) was born in Patrick County, Virginia, graduated from West Point in 1854, and afterwards served with the cavalry in Texas and Kansas. In 1861, he resigned his U.S. commission to become a colonel in the First Virginia Cavalry. He was made a general after First Manassas. Stuart was known for his style as well as for his accomplishments, which were both considerable. His plumed hat, dashing appearance, high spirits, and the habit of singing while riding were legendary. When placed at the head of Stonewall Jackson's troops after Jackson was wounded, he led the charge singing, "Won't you come out of the Wilderness," changing it to

"Now, Joe Hooker, won't you come out of the Wilderness," to suit the occasion. Stuart was also a bit of a flirt, writing lighthearted verses to any number of ladies, despite the fact that he was deeply devoted to his wife and two children. His splendid beard, which so enhanced his looks, he grew at the youngest possible age to disguise an abnormally receding chin. This supposed sign of weakness was also possibly the reason for his reckless disregard of physical danger. He was shot through the abdomen, during a battle at the Yellow Tavern near Richmond, fighting General Sheridan. Although in great pain, he refused a drink of brandy to dull it, because he had promised his mother never to touch spirits, and he was going to keep the promise. His last orders to his troops was a shout from the ambulance, rallying them with: "Go back and do your duty. I'd rather die than be whipped." He died the next day, May 12, 1864, at the age of thirty-one.

William Booth Taliaferro (1822-1898) was a native of Virginia, a lawyer and a politician. He fought under Jackson and commanded his old division, but his relationship with Jackson was not always smooth. After the war, General Taliaferro returned to Virginia where he served as a judge and a legislator.

Richard Taylor (1826-1879) was born in Kentucky and educated at Harvard and Yale. Before the Civil War, he lived in Louisiana and was active in state politics. His father was General and later President Zachary Taylor, and Confederate President Jefferson Davis was his brother-in-law. Gen. Taylor commanded a brigade in the Shenandoah Valley and Seven Days campaigns, and later fought in the West. His command was the last major force to surrender east of the Mississippi.

Rev. William Spotswood White was pastor of the Lexington Presbyterian Church from 1848 to 1867. White visited Jackson in the field several times during the war to preach to the troops. His son Hugh served under Jackson and was killed at Second Manassas. Rev. White was born in 1800 in Hanover County, Virginia, attended Hampden-Sydney and Union Theological Seminary and served in several parishes, including one in Charlottesville, where he also became a chaplain at the University of Virginia. (There he was a colleague of Dr. William Holmes McGuffey of the McGuffey's readers which sold over 120 million copies over the years.) White and his wife had five sons and two daughters. He was called to the Lexington Presbyterian church after this church went through a period of turmoil with its former pastor, Rev. Skinner. The congregation had 250 members, which included two doctors of divinity and five other Presbyterian ministers - no doubt due to its location in a town with two colleges. White's salary in Lexington was $900 per annum plus a manse. White was basically pro-Union, yet, like other Virginians, once the war started, he supported the Confederacy, saying: "I claimed the poor right of choosing whom to fight. Necessity was laid upon me... so I chose to become a rebel, but never a secessionist." White died shortly after his resignation from the Lexington pulpit.

William Henry Chase Whiting (1824-1865), native Mississippian, graduated at the top of his 1845 West Point class. His academic record was not exceeded until 1903 with the arrival of Douglas McArthur. As an upperclassman, Whiting adopted Jackson as his plebe, and helped him over rough academic spots. Whiting later served in the U.S. Army engineers until he resigned in 1861 to join the Confederacy. During the Valley campaign, General Lee sent Whiting to reinforce Jackson. Whiting found Jackson's modus operandi irritating and called Jackson a fool. Whiting was wounded and captured at Fort Fisher, North Carolina, in January 1865, and died in New York a prisoner on March 10, 1865.

Wirt Woodson (1831-1875), Jackson's half brother, turned out to be something of a black sheep. His lack of application, especially in the matter of studies, was sometimes attributed to his eating, as a child, buckeye chestnuts, considered to be poisonous. Jackson described him once: "His mind is unsettled and flying from thing to thing." Jackson tried to help him with advice, urging him to get an education and become a civil engineer. But Wirt told him he was not qualified for any occupation except farming, so Jackson considered giving him a thousand dollars to buy some land, but eventually it did not come to pass. Jackson continued urging Wirt to "go to some active occupation," while Wirt kept writing for money because he was robbed on a boat, or he put down a deposit on some land and lost it, or a horse ran away and he needed another one. At one time, Wirt went to California to make his fortune, and later he lived in Indiana. He married in 1863 and had seven children. He named his eldest one Thomas Warren for his two half brothers.

NOTES

Introduction, Old Jack
1. Lenoir Chambers, *Stonewall Jackson*, vol. I. p.56.
2. Jackson's eyes were blue and this probably refers to their penetrating otherwordly gaze.
3. Elizabeth Randolph Preston Allan, *A March Past*, p.121.

Chapter 1. Roots and Family
1. Chambers, I. p.44.
2. *Ibid.*, I. p.23. Jonathan Jackson had been nursing his six year old daughter Elizabeth who had typhoid fever. She died on March 6, 1826. After her funeral Jonathan came down with the same disease and succumbed to it on March 26. The next day, on March 27, his wife gave birth to a daughter, Laura Ann.
3. R.L. Dabney, *Life and Campaigns of Lieut.-Gen. Thomas J. Jackson*, pp. 11-14, says that all three Jackson children went together, when Tom was five years old, first to Mrs. White, one of their father's sisters, and then to the Brakes. From there Thomas ran away and made his way to the Jackson Mill and Uncle Cummins. Dabney also states that both Warren and Thomas lived with Cummins and that Warren at the age of fourteen rebelled and wanted to be on his own. Dabney then recounts the story of the two boys going to the Mississippi River, saying that Cummins made them both leave together to live with other relatives. Their adventure on the island followed because Warren would not submit himself to discipline at the other relatives' homes. However, most other historians disagree. The consensus is that Tom and Warren were split from the beginning. Laura stayed at the Jackson Mill up until after Grandmother Jackson died. Mrs. Jackson in her memoirs glosses over the details when and where the three children lived, except that they were eventually split and Tom was the only one with Cummins.
4. Mary Anna Jackson, *Memoirs of Stonewall Jackson*, p.13, also Dabney, p.14. where he describes Cummins: "As a friend he was steadfast and generous...and though slow to take offence, as an enemy he was equally bitter and unforgiving. He never had political aspirations for himself, but his unbounded influence usually gave the honors of his country to the person whom he favored. Yet his business morals, save when he was bound by his own voluntary promises, which he always sacredly fulfilled, were accounted unscrupulous; and he was passionately fond of litigation, that his legal controversies consumed a large part of the income of a liberal estate and the earnings of his own giant industry." Dabney may be hinting here at

the time when Cummins was involved in a fraudulent pension scheme and another time was charged with counterfeiting. And, he was sued even by his own mother who accused him of defrauding her of property left by her late husband.

5. Chambers, I. p.35. The advantage of Tom over Uncle Cummins as jockey may have been more because one was a slight youngster and the other one a 250 pound man. According to Dabney (p.20) Tom in his teens was of short stature for his age, favoring his father. It was not until West Point that he grew to his full height.

6. Thomas Jackson Arnold, *Early Life and Letters of General Thomas J. Jackson,* p.162, letter of July 6, 1850. Dabney, pp. 14-15, in his book writes that Tom was Cummins' favorite, and that this was what caused Warren's resentment and his decision to strike out on his own. Dabney, as well as other Jackson's biographers, also mention that Cummins treated Tom in many ways as an equal, not as a child. "He treated the little boy more as a companion than as child, ...imparting to him his plans and thoughts as though to an equal and counsellor, ...and always rather requesting than demanding his compliance with the discipline of his household. The child was thus stimulated in the work of his own self-government from a very early period, and left to an independence of action more suited for a man."

Chapter 2. A Most Independent Lad

1. Chambers, I. p.34.

2. Jackson, p. 23. The ages sixteen and twelve seem to be the accepted by most historians for this adventure, however Dabney (pp.15-16) writes that Warren was fourteen and Tom nine. He also mentions that the boys came down with 'ague' which is sort of malarial fever and chills.

3. Frank E. Vandiver, *Mighty Stonewall,* p.9.

4. Chambers, I. p.36. It was supposedly Peregrine Hays (son of Congressman Hays,) who went to school with him who made this remark. There is a record that Tom attended school of itinerant teachers at least four times. However this was seldom for more than a month or two. These teachers were as a rule barely more educated than their students. When Tom was fifteen he was fortunate to attend a school taught by Col. Alexander Withers, who was highly educated and well read and was an author of a book on early Indian wars. Tom attended his school for two months.

5. Vandiver, p.10.

6. Chambers, I. p.34.

7. *Ibid.,* I. p. 37.

8. *Ibid.,*I. p.42, also Jackson p. 28-9.

9. Jackson possibly could have gone to VMI, which was then in exist-

NOTES

ence but he may not known about it.

10. Vandiver, p.12.
11. Chambers, I. p.50.
12. *Ibid.*
13. *Ibid.*, The opportunity of attending West Point came in such a hurry that Tom left his accounts of a constable in disarray. Charges were made against them within the next year claiming that he had not accounted for some claims. Eventually this was settled with the help of Cummins.
14. *Ibid.*, I. p.53.
15. Jackson, p.32.
16. Holmes Moss Alexander, *The Hidden Years of Stonewall Jackson*, p.7. Because of the debts left by Tom's father the family lost the title to their house. They had to move to a much smaller place provided for them through the generosity of Jonathan Jackson's friends.
17. Arnold, p.131, letter of February 28, 1848.
18. Chambers, I. p.54.
19. Arnold, p.68, letter of February 10, 1845.

Chapter 3. Jackson at West Point

1. Dabney H. Maury, *Recollections of a Virginian*, p.22.
2. *Ibid.*
3. Chambers, I. p.55.
4. *Ibid.*, I. p.56.
5. *Ibid.*, I. p.60.
6. Vandiver, p.15.
7. Chambers, I. p.62, quoting Lloyd Lewis in *Capt. Sam Grant*. On the other hand Dabney (p.17) says, when writing about Jackson's early education, that, "Thomas showed no quickness of aptitude for any of his studies except arithmetic; in this he always outstripped his schoolmates, seemingly without effort."
8. Maury, p.22.
9. *Ibid.*, p.23.
10. Vandiver, p.15.
11. Jackson, p.25.
12. Vandiver, p.15.
13. Chambers, I. p.74. The dropout rate at West Point was sizeable. The class of 1846 started with 112 plebes. Four years later only 59 graduated. Overall it was a remarkable class. In addition to Jackson it contained 16 future generals, including, on the Federal side, McClellan, Foster, Reno, Stoneman, Couch and Gibbon, and on the Confederate side, Maury, D.R.

Jones, W.D.Smith, Wilcox, A.P. Hill and George Pickett, who finished at the bottom of the class. Pickett's low class standing resulted from disciplinary rather than academic problems. On the other hand Jackson's class standing was enhanced by the remarkably low number of demerits he collected, only 48 over the four years.

14. *Ibid.,* I. p.21.
15. Jackson, p.33.

Chapter 4. You May Be Whatever You Resolve to Be

1. Jackson, pp.35-38. Dabney (p.37) says that these maxims seemed to have been selected from books and in part adopted from Jackson's own experience. But he is concerned that, "It does not appear that Jackson was under the influence of vital Christianity at West Point."
2. Chambers, I. p.318.
3. *Ibid.,* I. p.563. The officer's name was Colonel Patton.
4. Chambers, I. p.76. Benny Havens was a favorite, albeit unauthorized and out of bounds, watering hole of the cadets near the West Point academy. Of the group of young officers, Botts died within six months in Mexico, and Wilson died in the 1850s in New Mexico. The other three all earned flag rank in the Confederate army.
5. Jackson, p.27.
6. Arnold, p.66.
7. Maury, p.23.
8. Chambers, I. p.70.
9. Henry Kyd Douglas, *I Rode With Stonewall,* p.234.
10. Jackson, p.35. However, there was a unsubstantiated rumor, listed in a manuscript by General Ezra Ayers kept in the Antietam Battlefied Commission Papers, and referred to by couple of Jackson's contemporaries, that as a West Point cadet on leave in Beverly, Jackson sired an illegitimate child. H.M. Alexander mentions it in his biography, while other current Jackson biographers omit it. Possibly Dabney, (pp.24-25), alludes to something: "..as young Jackson approached manhood, his conduct became somewhat irregular...he was an ardent frequenter of races, of house-raisings, and of country-dances."

Chapter 5. The Mexican War

1. Maury, p. 29, also Chambers I. p.82.
2. Arnold, p. 88, letter April 22, 1847.
3. Jackson, p.54.
4. *Ibid.*

NOTES

5. Arnold, p.85, letter March 30, 1847.
6. Chambers, I. p.90.
7. Arnold, p.91, letter May 25, 1847.
8. *Ibid.*
9. Chambers, I. p.96.
10. Arnold, p.93.
11. *Ibid.,* p.103.
12. Jackson, p.43.
13. Chambers, I. p.113.
14. *Ibid.,* p.114.
15. Jackson, p.45.
16. Arnold, p.115.
17. *Ibid.*
18. Jackson, p.44.
19. Chambers, I. p.141.
20. Arnold, p.119.
21. *Ibid.,* p.136, letter March 23, 1848.
22. Chambers, I. p.145.
23. Arnold, p.135, letter March 23, 1848.
24. *Ibid.*, p.132, letter February 28, 1848.
25. *Ibid.*
26. *Ibid.,* p.167.
27. *Ibid.,* p.129, letter October 26, 1847.

Chapter 6. A Soldier in Peacetime

1. Chambers, I. p.164. On his baptismal record Jackson's name is listed, erroneously, as Thomas Jefferson Jackson.

2. Jackson, p.382. In Jackson's circles the majority of people held deep prejudices against the Catholic faith. Dabney mentions with something akin to surprise that Jackson "..said that the (Catholic) system, as expounded by intelligent Romanists, was by no means so gross or so obnoxious to common sense as is represented by the mass of decided Protestants." Dabney, p.56.

3. Arnold, pp.145-6.

4. Chambers, I. p.153. Dabney (p.20) speaking of Tom's early teens mentions, "..his constitution, even then, gave signs of infirmity. An obscure disease of the stomach and other organs of nutrition had seized upon him, harassing him with chronic irritations or prostrations of the nerves, sleepless nights, and lassitude. A year or two later, notwithstanding the means used to re-establish his constitution, these symptoms assumed the more ominous form of a slight paralysis.. the latter, however, wore away after a time."

5. *Ibid.,* I. p.165.
6. *Ibid.,* I. p.63.
7. Arnold, p.72, letter November 25, 1845.
8. *Ibid.,* p.134, letter March 21, 1848. Others disagreed. A.P. Hill thought Mexican climate was unhealthy.
9. Vandiver, p.182, also Douglas.
10. Arnold, p.155, letter July 2, 1849.
11. Alexander, p.80. It was at this time that Jackson received the healthfood diet from his physician. He followed it more or less for the rest of his life. It was also at this time that he visited, near Fort Ontario, for the first time a 'water cure establishment.'
12. Arnold, p.154, letter July 2, 1849.
13. Chambers, I. p.156. During his tour of duty at Fort Hamilton Jackson visited West Point. His former classmates George McClellan and Dabney Maury were instructors there at that time. The description of Jackson's health problems was written about forty years later by Maury.
14. Chambers, I. p.389.
15. Arnold, p.155, letter July 2, 1849.
16. Vandiver, p.50.
17. Chambers, I. p.160.
18. *Ibid.,* pp.160-1. It is not certain whether or not Jackson played cards for money, i.e. gambled. This was extremely common in the army so it is possible. However, in later years when Jackson joined the Presbyterian Church he would not engage in card playing, or dancing, as the Presbyterians considered it sinful and forbade it.

Chapter 7. A Mistaken Sense of Duty
1. Arnold, p. 169, letter March 1, 1851.
2. *Ibid.*
3. Chambers, I. p.182.
4. *Ibid.,* I. pp.188-91.
5. *Ibid.,* I. p.185.
6. *Ibid.,* I. pp.194-5.
7. *Ibid.,* I. p.199.
8. Dabney, p.60.
9. Jackson, p.51.

Chapter 8. Lexington and VMI
1. Jackson, p.55.

NOTES 141

2. Allen Tate, Stonewall Jackson, p.49, also similar in Chambers, I. p.226.

3. Chambers, I. p.228, and Dabney, p.65. VMI's superintendent, Col. Smith, agreed. Some years later he remarked: "He was a brave man, a conscientious man and a good man, but he was no professor."

4. *Ibid.*, I. p.227.

5. Jackson, p.62.

6. Chambers, I. p.271. Dabney, p.73 writes that Jackson would get up several times during the evening's program to deliver his speech, "At a suitable moment he would rise again, and renew his effort, perhaps to end with a similar painful halt."

7. Tate, p.54.

8. *Ibid.*, p.50.

9. *Ibid.*

10. Chambers, I. p.237.

11. *Ibid.*

12. *Ibid.*, I. p.224.

13. *Ibid.*, I. p.231.

14. *Ibid.*

15. *Ibid.*, I. p.228.

16. *Ibid.*, I., quoting Maury.

17. *Ibid.*, I. p.230, also Arnold p.176.

Chapter 9. Home Life In Lexington

1. Arnold, p.190 and p.186.

2. Jackson, p.63.

3. *Ibid.*

4. Chambers, I. p.224.

5. Vandiver, p.85.

6. Chambers, I. p.236.

7. Jackson, p.60.

8. Chambers, I. p.225. It was Jackson's sister-in-law Maggie Junkin who made this remark and noted it in her journal.

9. Vandiver, p.86.

10. *Ibid.*, p.90.

11. *Ibid.*, p.85.

12. *Ibid.*, p.89, also Chambers I. p.226.

13. Arnold, p.199, letter April 15, 1853. Jackson may have been so enthusiastic about the party because this was shortly before his marriage to Ellie. He no doubt expected to see her there.

14. Jackson, p.64.

15. Chambers, I. p.243.
16. *Ibid.,* I. p.244.
17. Vandiver, p.88.
18. Jackson, p.77.
19. *Ibid.,* p.59.
20. Vandiver pp.90-91, also Chambers I. p.248.
21. Allan, p.120.
22. Jackson, p.99.
23. Allan, p.122.
24. *Ibid.,* p.91. The 'unfortunate episode' does not refer to Jackson. It was some other young man whom Maggie met before the family moved to Lexington.
25. *Ibid.,* p.93. According to the contemporary accounts J.T.L. Preston was a handsome and captivating man. There is every evidence that Maggie found him attractive. She agreed to marry him even though the date of their wedding was less than two years after the death of his first wife - which she, along with the contemporary society, considered rash and slightly improper.

Chapter 10. Second Marriage

1. Arnold, p.246, letter July 9, 1856.
2. Jackson, p.99.
3. *Ibid.*
4. *Ibid.,* p.100.
5. *Ibid.*
6. Arnold, p. 254. The letter is undated, and it says: "I will begin by stating that I have an invitation for you; and what do you think it is? and who from? For it is not often that I am authorized to send you invitations, and especially pressing ones. And I suppose you begin to think, or may think, Well, what does he mean? Why doesn't he tell me at once and be done with it? Well, you see I have finished the first page of my letter. . . .Well, now, having cultivated your patience a little, as all woman are said to have curiosity, I will tell you that Miss Mary Anna Morrison, a friend of mine, in the western part of North Carolina, and in the southern part of the state, is engaged to be married to an acquaintance of yours living in this village, and she has requested me to urge you to attend her wedding in July next. . . . .I told her that I would give the invitation, and having done so, feel that I am free from all further responsibility in the matter. I told her that I didn't think that you would be able to accept it, and if you can't, just let me know in your next (sic), and transfer the invitation to your humble servant, and he will not decline; for he is very anxious to go, as he is much interested in the ceremony and the occasion, and the young lady is a very special friend of mine."

NOTES

7. Chambers, I. p.279.
8. Jackson, p.103.
9. *Ibid.*, p.105.
10. *Ibid.*, p.107. They bought the house from a local physician Dr. Archibald Graham. It was much too large for them, but at that time there were few if any houses for sale in town. They had plans of eventually building themselves a new house.
11. *Ibid.*, p.71.
12. *Ibid.*, p.106. Mrs. Jackson wrote her memoirs some thirty years after the death of her husband. It is possible, and even probable, that she may have forgotten some of the less harmonious moments of her marriage.
13. *Ibid.*, p.109.
14. Allan, p.121.
15. Jackson, p.119.
16. *Ibid.*, p.138. Anna was in North Carolina at that time attending a wedding of her sister.
17. *Ibid.*, p.110.
18. *Ibid.*, p.47.
19. Arnold, pp.257-8, letter December 1857.
20. *Ibid.*
21. *Ibid.*, pp.265-6, letter August 18, 1858.
22. *Ibid.*, p.195.
23. Jackson, p.134.
24. *Ibid.*, p.71.
25. *Ibid.*
26. *Ibid.*, pp.128-9. He wrote to Anna what the family servants were doing, commenting that Hetty took such a good care of hilling the celery that he did not interfere in it, as not to spoil it.
27. Arnold, p.162, letter July 6, 1850. Dabney in his book mentions (p. 15,) that Jackson as a child lived in a household with slaves: "He (Cummins Jackson) owned a valuable farm and mills, and was one of the largest slaveholders in the county of Lewis."
28. Chambers, I. p.47.
29. *Ibid.*, I. p.37, also Tate, p. 11.
30. Jackson, p.114.
31. Chambers, I. p.289.
32. Jackson, p.207. Jackson used exactly the same words when writing about it to Maggie Preston. It was Maggie Preston who kept an eye on the Jackson servants in Lexington during the war. Jackson's wife was living then with her parents in North Carolina and took home with her only Hetty.
33. Jackson, p.119.

34. Tate, p.13.

35. Jackson, p.207. Anna wrote in her memoirs: "At his request I taught them - i.e. Hetty's two sons - to read."

36. Tate, p.40.

37. Jackson, pp.142-3.

38. Arnold, p. 244, letter June 6, 1856. Note: Jackson's salary at VMI was $1,200 when he started. It may have been somewhat higher five years later. If he had sufficient savings to plan a purchase of two or three thousand acres of land selling then at a dollar an acre, he must have saved about half of his earnings totalling $6,000 to $6,500 over the five years.

39. *Ibid.*, p.252.

40. Jackson House Manuscript- *Stonewall in Lexington.*

41. Letter, August 1860. Furniture could be expensive. In her inventory Mrs. Jackson valued their sofa at $60, one bureau at $70 another at $50, and the parlor carpet $100. The piano valued at $500 they purchased in New York in the summer of 1858.

42. Arnold, pp.286-7, letter September 1860.

43. According to Lenoir Chambers Jackson's library probably had more than 100 volumes, some 90 of them can be found now in the Battle Abbey in Richmond. Others had been given by Mrs. Jackson as souvenirs to his old comrades in arms. In the Jackson book collection were many of the textbooks he used while student at West Point, as well the textbooks he used while teaching at VMI. He also had a number of military volumes, few probably acquired during the Civil War. A large group consisted of religious books, including some in French. This also included the Principles of Courtesy, which was heavily marked and underlined. The most numerous were books about history and general literature. These included histories of the United States, England and France as well as Ancient History, collected works of Shakespeare, Milton's works, Pilgrim's Progress, Plutarch's Lives, British Painters and Sculptors, copies of Apostles and Early Martyrs, History of Jews, and Life of Mohammed. He had several travel books, mostly acquired for his European trip. In addition he had several books on health, including The New Hydropathic Day Book, with Recipes for Cooking on Hygienic Principles (1853) and Fowler; On Memory, and a well used and marked The Family Kitchen Gardener.

44. Jackson, p.63.

45. *Ibid.*, p.43.

46. Jackson, p.206.

Chapter 11. To Arms
1. Arnold, p.292.

NOTES

2. Jackson, p.139.
3. Chambers, II. p.342. This family division was not rare. Even President Lincoln had four brothers-in-law in the Confederate army and three of his sisters-in-law were married to Confederate officers. As a result of this the president's wife Mary Todd Lincoln was often accused of being a Southern spy.
4. Vandiver pp.131-2.
5. Alexander, p.141, quoting Virginius Dabney in *"Richmond."*
6. Vandiver, p.134.
7. Jackson, p.150, also Chambers, I. p.317.
8. Arnold, pp. 86-7.
9. Alexander, p.161. (According to other sources, in particular Lenoir Chambers, Bee's exhortation was first described in the Charleston Mercury on July 25, 1861: "There is Jackson standing like a stone-wall. Let us determine to die here and we will conquer. Follow me." The article as a whole was not in praise of Jackson, but a homage to the bravery of General Bee. The information was later reprinted by other newspapers. The name of Stonewall did not catch on immediately with the general public, mostly because Jackson's name was not appearing at that time in the newspapers. However, only three days after the battle, on July 24, the diarist and author Mary Boykin Chesnut quoted in her diary her husband's letter where he said he had taken orders to Jackson, "whose regiment stood so stock still under fire that they were called a Stone-Wall."
10. Jackson, pp.178-9, letter August 5, 1861.
11. Vandiver, p.142.
12. Chambers, II. pp.95-6.
13. Jackson, p.171.

Chapter 12. Family Life in War
1. Jackson, p.170.
2. *Ibid.,* p.183.
3. *Ibid.,* p.184.
4. *Ibid.,* p.190.
5. *Ibid.,* p.182.
6. *Ibid.,* p.200, letter November 4, 1861.
7. *Ibid.,* p.210, letter November 16, 1861.
8. *Ibid.,* pp.211-12.
9. *Ibid.*
10. Vandiver, p.191.
11. Arnold, p. 263, letter June 1858

12. Jackson, p. 363, letter December 10, 1862.

13. Vandiver, p. 191

14. W. G. Bean, *Stonewall's Man - Sandie Pendleton*, p.108. The hat from which the gold ribbon came had been a gift from Mrs. Jackson to her husband. He later apologized to her for giving the ribbon away, telling her the lace was too much for him, "that he preferred simplicity". According to Dabney, p.640., little Janie died of scarlet fever.

15. Arnold, p. 305, letter February 1860.

16. Ibid., p. 360.

17. Tate, p. 282.

18. Jackson, p.360. The announcement was made by Anna's sister Harriet Irwin, writing in the name of the child. It went in part: " My own dear Father, as my mother's letter has been cut short by my arrival, I think it but justice that I should continue it.....I am a very tiny little thing, I weigh only eight and a half pounds, and Aunt Harriet says I am the express image of my darling papa. My aunts both say that I am a little beauty. My hair is dark and long, my eyes are blue, my nose straight just like papa's, and my complexion not all red like most young ladies of my age, but a beautiful blending of the lily and the rose. Now, this would sound very vain if I were older, but I assure you that I have not a particle of feminine vanity, my only desire in life being to nestle in close to my mama, to feel her soft caressing touch, and to drink in the pearly stream provided by kind Providence for my support. My mother is very comfortable this morning. She is anxious to have my name decided upon, and hopes you will write and give me a name, with your blessing. ....Your dear little wee Daughter."

19. *Ibid.*, p.400, letter February 3, 1853.

20. *Ibid.*

21. *Ibid.*, p.407.

22. *Ibid.*, p.409.

23. *Ibid.*

24. *Ibid.*, p.363. To reassure his wife he wrote her: "Give the baby-daughter a shower of kisses from her father, and tell her he loves her better than all the baby-boys in the world." Actually Jackson did desire a son but according to Mrs. Jackson it was because he believed that "men had a larger sphere of usefulness than women." Once his daughter was born he said he preferred a daughter, since God so ordained it, and, as Anna wrote, "His will was entirely in subjection to that of his Heavenly Father."

25. *Ibid.*, p.399.

26. *Ibid.*, p.411.

27. *Ibid.*, p.413.

28. *Ibid.*

29. *Ibid.* Note: In the battle of Chancellorsville the Union general 'Fighting Joe' Hooker was planning to defeat Lee's army by circling him and attacking him from the side and in his rear - thus forcing Lee to retreat right into the hands of Hooker's main forces. The difficulty was that to do this Hooker had to move fifty thousand troops across two rivers, the Rappahannock and the Rapidan, do it fast, and without being discovered. The terrain also was not hospitable to the Union forces. They had to go through the Wilderness, a thick, impenetrable overgrown forest, which was not at all suited for movement of heavy guns nor for battles with large number of men. It was much more suited for hit and run skirmishes favored by the smaller forces of the Confederates. Hooker had some 133,000 men, while Lee had only 62,000. As it happened, through carelessness and overconfidence the Union forces did not anticipate a Confederate attack. They thought that Lee's forces were retreating. But in the evening of May 2, 1863, before they could get into a position in a more open country, they were routed by 28,000 men under Stonewall Jackson. Hooker at his headquarters in Chancellorsville was unaware what happened until the first disorganized men came back. The various Union troops quickly tried to respond to the attack, but by this time there was confusion with groups of men from both sides scattered through the woods and skirmishing in the dark. It was in this confusing period that Stonewall Jackson, on a scouting mission ahead of the lines, was accidently wounded by men from a North Carolina infantry regiment. During the rest of the night both armies engaged in a hellish melee killing probably as many of their own men as the enemy. The next day the slaughter continued. Hooker was slightly wounded as he was standing on the porch of his headquarters in Chancellorsville - a shot had split a wooden pillar against which he was leaning, stunning him. Fighting continued for two more days, but although the Union forces still outnumbered the Confederates both in men and equipment, General Hooker failed to take the initiative. Years later when he was asked what went wrong he answered: "Well, to tell the truth, I just lost confidence in Joe Hooker."

Chapter 13. Stonewall Jackson's Way

1. Chambers, II. p.331.
2. Written by John Williamson Palmer.
3. Douglas, p.70.
4. Vandiver, p.290.
5. Jackson, p.586, in an essay by Col. Henderson. Note: The first battle of Manassas was on July 21, 1861. In it Union General Irvin McDowell's forces, some 35,000 strong, tried to capture Richmond and make a quick

end to the war. General P.G.T. Beauregard who commanded the Confederate forces had 22,000 men. Most Washingtonians believed that the Confederates would cave in. They drove out of Washington with picnic hampers to watch the spectacle. However, McDowell's troops were new recruits, and their march from Washington was slow. This gave an opportunity to the Confederate forces to rush in General Joseph E. Johnston's 10,000 men from the Shenandoah Valley (including Jackson). When the fighting started it was heavier than expected, and although the Confederate forces were hard pressed, and possibly at times in danger of defeat, they held the ground. Each side waited for more reinforcements. Eventually McDowell's raw recruits were spent and started retreating across Bull Run Creek, where they found the road jammed by fleeing spectators trying to get back to the capital. A Confederate shell hit the road and panic ensued. It is possible that had Jackson been able to attack at this point he could have gone on to take Washington. As it was, by the next morning, July 22, 1861, McDowell's army was safely back in Washington.

6. Chambers, II. p.330.
7. Douglas, p.21.
8. *Ibid.,* p.70.
9. Chambers, I. p.566.
10. *Ibid.,* II. p.13.
11. Douglas, p.235.
12. Tate, p.163.
13. *Ibid.,* p.201.
14. Douglas, p.235.
15. Jackson, p.285.
16. Douglas, p.40.
17. Jackson, pp.304-5.
18. Vandiver, p.275. The first Sabbath Jackson had to give up to the Civil War was April 21, 1861, when he was ordered to march the VMI cadets to Richmond.
19. Jackson, p.248.
20. *Ibid.,* p.287.
21. Douglas, pp.154-5.
22. Bourke Davis, *The Civil War: Strange and Fascinating Facts,* p.242. Clairborne Mason was a colorful character. He never learned how to read or write, except for signing his name, yet he was a successful builder and contractor. With a small pocket rule he would sight a hillside or a grade and from it accurately estimate the amount of earth to be moved. Once Jackson needed a long bridge so that he could reach the enemy. He asked Mason how long it would take him to build it. Mason said: "General give me two

NOTES 149

hundred men, and I'll have you over in twenty-four hours." So Jackson ordered his corps of engineers to draw the plans and assigned Mason the men. The next day, to the hour, Mason reported. "General the bridge is ready. But the plans are not here yet."
    23. Tate, p.224.
    24. Vandiver, p.254.
    25. *Ibid.,* p.250.
    26. Chambers, I. pp.69-70. Dabney (pp.38-39,) describes in detail this episode especially the doubtful character of the wayward cadet, Thomas McLean from Missouri, who was supposed to have come from much the same background as Jackson, was also an orphan, with a weak early education, and who, "Like Jackson had incurred the sportive malice of the students on his arrival at the Academy." But later, "...he disclosed laxity of principle, told less than the truth in order to evade 'demerits,' and contracted degrading associations in the neighboring village." After the affair with Jackson's rifle "It was not long before his opponent (i.e. McLean) was under arrest for disgraceful conduct, violated his parole, and was expelled on that account, a short time before he would have graduated." Dabney notes that the young man then went to Texas to study law, but not prospering at it went to California, tried to swindle the captain of the ship of his fare was put ashore at Mazatlan. "There he wandered into the mountains and, and attached himself to a roving tribe of the Tuscon Indians, among whom his skill in savage warfare, robbery, and murder, raised him to a sort of chieftainship, and the possession of half-a-dozen tawny wives." He quarreled with the Indians over a murder of a poor pedlar, and the tribe expelled him too.
    27. Douglas, p. 266.
    28. Tate, pp.128-9.
    29. Jackson, p.606, in an essay by Maj. Gen. M.C.Butler,
    30. Maury, p.71. Note: Dabney Maury was Jackson's classmate at West Point. They fought together also in Mexico. Jackson's charges against General Richard Garnett were that he allowed the 1st Brigade to fall back during the battle of Kernstown, in April 1862, exposing another brigade's flank and causing them to fall back. Afterwards Jackson relieved Garnett of his command and preferred charges in anticipation of a court martial. The general opinion was that Garnett was an able and brave officer and fell back only to prevent further losses because his men were out of ammunition. General Garnett was reassigned to another command, and eventually cleared of the charges. He died at Gettysburg. General Charles S. Winder (West Point class 1850), was a strict and demanding officer, a martinet. He was put in charge

of the Stonewall Brigade after General Garnett was removed from its command. He was not welcomed by the brigade's officers or men. Winder's difficulties with Jackson seemed to have been in the early days of his command, when there were rumors that Jackson had put him under arrest for not bringing up his brigade fast enough. In later engagements the relationship between Jackson and Winder was more harmonious. When Winder was killed by an enemy bullet at Cedar Run in August 1862, Jackson wrote about him: "It is difficult to do justice to the merits of this accomplished officer." And to Anna Jackson he wrote: "I can hardly think of the fall of Brigadier-General C.S. Winder, without tearful eyes." However, Winder's troops were relieved. Apparently some of them, who had been punished by the general for straggling, had planned to kill him in the next battle.

31. Chambers, II. p.331.

32. *Ibid.,* II. pp.180-1. Jackson had been unhappy with Hill for some time, at least since the Second Manassas. Jackson was bothered that Hill's troops started marches later than he had ordered, that there were too many stragglers and what he considered general lack of discipline. This latest incident, on September 4, 1862, was precipitated when Jackson gave orders to one of Hill's division to halt. Hill came over, chewed out the brigade commander, and when told by him that Jackson gave the order, Hill turned to Jackson.

33. Douglas, p.196.

34. Arnold, p.169, letter March 1, 1851. Dabney (p.25,) writes "It is manifest that his nature was intensely ambitious and aspiring," and "He knew himself to be a depressed scion of a noble and influential stock."

35. Vandiver, p.289.

36. Jackson, p.167.

37. *Ibid.,* p.161.

38. Dabney, p.247. quotes this letter to Anna as; "It gives my heart an additional gratification to read a letter that hasn't travelled on our holy Sabbath. I am very thankful to that good God who withholds no good thing from me (though I am so utterly unworthy and so ungrateful), for making me a major-general of the provisional army of the Confederate States. The commission dates from October 7th. What I need is a more grateful heart to the 'giver of every good and perfect gift,' I have great reason to be thankful to our God for all His mercies which He has bestowed, and continues to shower upon me...."

39. Douglas, p.15, also Vandiver, p.174.

40. Chambers, I. pp.431-41. Apparently Loring went over Jackson's head to Secretary Benjamin because he did not want to spend the winter in

NOTES

head to Secretary Benjamin because he did not want to spend the winter in the mountains. Winter campaigns were seldom attempted at that time. However, Jackson was in favor of them and had plans for Loring and his men. Jackson thought that winter campaigns were often effective and besides they were healthier for the troops than having them sit in winter quarters.

41. Vandiver, p.406. If General Lee had any doubts about Jackson's abilities in the early part of the war he certainly shed them later. The two generals developed an understanding of each other's military strategies, and Lee began to trust Jackson's judgment. By spring 1863 Lee said, "he wished he had many Jacksons." As a corps commander Jackson had four divisions under him led by Generals William B. Taliaferro, Richard S. Ewell, A.P. Hill and D.H. Hill.

42. Chambers, I. p.398. Major Imboden asked him this question.

43. Arnold, p.196. Dabney p.52, mentions Jackson's remarks on how he felt under fire in Mexico. In a rather curious way Dabney then draws a comparison between Jackson and Napoleon's lieutenant Marshal Ney - who according to Napoleon - "..was worth little as a general, saw nothing, and could do nothing, till he was enveloped in fire and smoke. Then he was all energy, sagacity, genius."

44. Douglas, pp.113-4.

45. Arnold, p.196.

46. Jackson, p.264, also Chambers, II. p.14.

Chapter 14. Jackson and Fame

1. Jackson, p.605, from essay by General Butler.
2. Vandiver, p.412.
3. Chambers, II. p.336.
4. Jackson, p.336.
5. Tate, p.225.
6. Jackson, p.330.
7. Douglas, p.121.
8. Jackson, p.184.
9. *Ibid.*, p.347.
10. *Ibid.*, p.302.
11. *Ibid.*, p.163.
12. Tate, p.255.
13. *Ibid.*, pp.255-6. Maj. Heros von Borcke was a Prussian volunteer. He wrote a memoir of his war experiences.
14. Vandiver, p.413. To Jackson's contemporaries the comparison of him with Cromwell came easily, as they were familiar with the historical

reputation of this English Puritan leader and Lord Protector whose military exploits against Charles I. were as well known as his religious beliefs. However Dabney, p. 113, took exception to it. He wrote that Cromwell's religion was essentially fanatical, and that he suffered from "selfish ambition" while Jackson was more spiritual.

15. Arnold, p.176.
16. Allen, p.77.
17. Chambers, I. p.233.
18. Douglas, pp.234-5.
19. Allen, p.123, letter December 5, 1861.
20. Chambers I. p.22, and II. p.344.
21. Douglas, p.196.
22. Chambers I. p.399. This discussion may have led to Imboden's question why Jackson had no fear in battle. See Ch. 13, footnote 41.
23. Tate, p.135.
24. Chambers, II. pp.182-3.
25. Douglas, p.20.
26. Chambers, II. p.146. Drinking was a problem on both sides of the conflict and both Union and Confederate commands had to fight against it. But this was difficult, because not only the enlisted men but the officers too were often drunk. One military chaplain ruefully remarked that many men who would not touch liquor at home thought that drinking in the army was all right if not downright essential. The senior commanders realized that most men in military jails and many in the hospitals were there because of drinking. Orders and directives from military headquarters on the subject were frequently sent to the different commands with predictable outcomes. If there was no liquor to be had the men would not drink, if liquor was available, which was most of the time, they would.
27. Douglas, p.148, also Tate, p.225.
28. *Ibid.,* p.186. Unlike Jackson Douglas did not drink alcoholic beverages because, as he said, he did not like the taste of it.
29. Tate, pp.185-6, letter August 18, 1858.
30. Douglas, p.20. Here Dabney, (p.14,) disagrees with his contemporaries. He writes, "He (Jackson) lived absolutely without any stimulant; using neither tea, coffee, tobacco or wine." Since Dabney was a clergyman who spent only a very short time serving under Jackson, it is likely that he was overcome by his desire to paint Jackson only in the best light. With the exception of tobacco, Jackson was known to use tea and coffee and in some instances even spirits.

NOTES

Chapter 15. His Time Had Come

1. Vandiver, p.478, also Chambers, II. p.414. Jackson was not the only one wounded in this volley. Jackson's engineer officer Captain Keith Boswell was mortally wounded and several couriers and signalmen were killed. Jackson's brother-in-law Joseph Morrison saved his own life by throwing himself from his horse in order to avoid the fire.

2. *Ibid.,* also Chambers, II. p.416.This was the same General Hill who was in September stripped of his command by Jackson. At Chancellorsville they were both fighting under Lee. As a senior general present it fell to Hill to take over Jackson's command. Unfortunately he was hit on his foot and disabled just a few minutes later while he was accompanying Jackson to the ambulance.

3. *Ibid.,* p.417, also Chambers II. p.480.

4. *Ibid.,* p.480. The three officers who accompanied Jackson all the way to the ambulance were his brother-in-law Joseph Morrison, Captain Benjamin Watkins Leigh, and Jackson's aide, Captain James Power Smith. Jackson was fond of Smith. He asked him to be his aide during the Maryland campaign when Smith was just a corporal and had little military experience. Smith was a son of a Presbyterian minister and studied for the ministry himself before the Civil War. After the war he had a long career as a Presbyterian minister. Smith stayed with the general during his final illness.

5. *Ibid.,* p.483, also Chambers, II. p.420.

6. Bean, p.116. There was some disagreement as to why Stuart was given the command. The decision to do it was probably made by General Hill. The command should have gone to General Robert E. Rodes. Although Rodes was only a brigadier general he was a good and able officer, and certainly more familiar with commanding infantry than a cavalry officer like Jeb Stuart.

7. Vandiver, p.484, also Chambers, II. p.423.

8. Tate, p.277.

9. Chambers, II. p.437.

10. *Ibid.,* II. p.438.

11. Jackson, p.450.

12. *Ibid.,* pp.451-2.

13. Vandiver, p.493, also Chambers, II. p.443.

14. Jackson, pp.454-6.

15. *Ibid.,* p.457.

Chapter 16. Return to Lexington

1. Jackson, p.305, also Bean pp.118-9.

2. Bean, pp.118-119.
3. *Ibid.,* p. 120.
4. *Ibid.,* p.106. Shortly after Jackson's death the Confederate War Department officially named Jackson's 1st Virginia Brigade as Stonewall Brigade. It was the only one of its type to get its nickname officially accepted.
5. From Davis.

NOTE:

Because of the flow of the narrative I have tried to limit footnotes generally only to quotes. At times quotations have been paraphrased except for passages where the exact wording seemed essential for accuracy or for period flavor.

BIBLIOGRAPHY

Information for the book came from a number of sources. Most of the incidents included here had been mentioned by several authors, sometimes with slightly different details. The following bibliography lists some of the more comprehensive sources, especially those which are easily available. There are many others.

Alexander, Holmes Moss, *The Hidden Years of Stonewall Jackson.* West Virginia Press Club, 1981. This is an episodic biography, almost psychoanalytic in tone. It does not have bibliography or index.

Allan, Elizabeth Randolph Preston, *Life and Letters of Margaret Junkin Preston.* This is a charming book, now out of print, by Maggie Preston's step daughter.

Arnold, Thomas Jackson, *Early Life and Letters of General Thomas J. Jackson.* This has been reissued and is available. The tone of the book is extremely adulatory, yet gives us the closest look at Jackson himself because it includes most of the letters, albeit often edited, he wrote to his sister Laura and her family.

Bean, W.G., *Sandie Pendleton-Stonewall's Man.* Gives a view of how young, staff members saw Jackson.

Chambers, Lenoir, *Stonewall Jackson,* vols. I & II. Broadfoot Publ. Co., 1959. This is a most comprehensive work available on Jackson. It covers in detail both his private and his military life. Chambers is a great-grandson of Rev. Drury Lacy who married Jackson and Anna.

Dabney, R. L., *Life and Campaigns of Lieut.-gen. Thomas J. Jackson.* First published in England before the end of the Civil War, it was expanded and published in the United States in 1866. The work has been the source for most biographies about Jackson. Even Anna Jackson is quoting long passages of it verbatim in her book published some thirty years later. Dabney in his preface to the book says that his "prime object has been to portray and vindicate his (Jackson's) Christian character..," He also mentions that the reader will notice "a certain polemic tone..... and while strict truthfulness has been studied, candid expression has been given to the feelings natural to a participant in the recent struggle."

Davis, Bourke, *The Civil War: Strange and Fascinating Facts.* The Fairfax Press, N.Y. 1982. It contains many interesting and curious nuggets of information about both sides of the war.

Douglas, Henry Kyd, *I Rode With Stonewall.* University of North Carolina Press, 1986. This has been reissued in paperback. Douglas is a good reporter. His book conveys both a young and independent view of the action and his admiration of Jackson.

Jackson, Mary Anna, *Memoirs of "Stonewall" Jackson.* Prentice Press,1895, reprinted in 1976 in Dayton, Ohio, Morningside Bookshop. This is the book that Jackson's widow wrote primarily to set the record straight and counter some of the more bizarre things written about her late husband. Although the tone can be at times too reverential it is a very human and warm tribute to the man and it tells us much about the woman he had married. It is generally accepted that Mrs. Jackson did not write the book on her own, she had a ghost writer or at least an extensive editor in the form of Dr. H. M. Field.The book also incorporates, often verbatim, much of the material covered in Dabney's classical biography of Jackson which was published shortly after the end of the Civil War.

Maury, Dabney H., *Recollections of a Virginian.* Maury was a witty and lively writer and his view of Jackson is affectionate but without awe. The book is unfortunately out of print.

Shoop, Michael I., *The Genealogies of the Jackson, Junkin & Morrison Families.* Historic Lexington Foundation, Va. 1981.

Tate, Allen, *Stonewall Jackson.* U of Michigan Press, 1957 (Copyright 1928) Tate writes with a Southern point of view. This is not a scholarly work, it contains no index, but it tells a number of interesting incidents described in a lively narrative.

Vandiver, Frank E., *Mighty Stonewall.* McGraw-Hill, 1957. Comprehensive, scholarly, the emphasis is on military history.

INDEX

Albert, (slave in the Jackson's household), 62
Allan, Elizabeth Preston, 53, 131
Alum Springs, 59, 62, 115
Amazing Grace, 63
Amy, (slave in the Jackson's household), 62
Ansted, 2
Antietam, (battle), 116, 120, 138
Appomattox, 120
Arnold, Grace, (TJJ's niece), 77-78, 117
Arnold, Jonathan, (TJJ's brother-in-law), 30, 117
Arnold, Laura, (nee Jackson, TJJ's sister), childhood 2, 5; writes TJJ, 9-10, 23; 26, disapproves of TJJ's behavior, 27-28; TJJ visits her, 30; suffers eye problems, 33; 34, 52, 54-55, 58-59, seeds from TJJ 61; 65, 66, 68, becomes Union sympathizer, 69; her children, 78; TJJ shops for wine, 101, 115, 117, 135
Arnold, Thomas, (TJJ's nephew), 28, 30, 39; in Lexington, 78, 117, 121
Ashby, Turner, 3
Asia, steamship, 54
Augusta County, 80
Banks, N.P., (Union general), 82, 85, 87, 116
Barney, Dr, Larry, 32-33
Bath County, 30
Battle Abbey (in Richmond), 144
battles, Civil War, (see also individual battles), first Manassas (Bull Run), 33, 34, 66, 71, 91, 99, 115, 118, 147; Seven Days, 34, 116, 132; Second Manassas, 84, 100, 116; Valley Campaign, 85; Cross Keys and Port Republic, 85, 116; Chancellorsville, 102-104, 116
Beauregard, Pierre G.T., (Confederate general), 72, 148
Bee, Bernard E., at Chapultepec, 25; at first Manassas, 71, 115, 117, 145
Benjamin, Judah P., (Confederate Secretary of War), 91, 150
Benny Haven's, 18, 138
Beverly, 27, 30, 115, 138
Bible Society, 49, 115
Boswell, Keith (Capt.), 153
Botts, Archibald Blair, 18, 138
Brake, Isaac, (TJJ's uncle), 3, 23, 118, 135
Brattleboro, 60, 115
Brockenbrough, John W., (Judge), 46, 120
Brown, John, (execution of), 115
Brown's Hotel, 18
Bull Run, see Manassas
Butcher, Gibson, 7-8
Camargo, 21
Cedar Mountain, (battle), 116, 150
Century Magazine, 71
Chambers, Lenoir, 41, 144
Chancellorsville, 102-104, 116, 147, 153
Chandler, Thomas, 105, 109
Chapultepec (battle), 25
Charlotte, N.C., 113
Cherubusco, (battle), 26, 114
Chesnut, Mary Boykin, 145
Christian, Julia Laura, (later Preston, TJJ's granddaughter), 113, 118
Christian, Susan, 113
Christian, Thomas Jonathan Jackson, (TJJ's grandson), 113, 118
Christian, William E., (Julia Jackson's husband), 113, 119
Church, James C. and his family, 35
Clarksburg, 1, 3, 9, 114, 123
Confederate bonds, 67
Contreras, (battle), 26, 114
Corbin family, 78, 130, 146
Corbin, Janie, 78, 130, 146
Cottage Home, 55
Cross Keys, (battle), 85, 116
Cyrus, (slave in the Jackson's household), 62, 63
Dabney, R.L., on TJJ in Florida, 39; on TJJ's teaching, 41; on TJJ's temper, 88; 90, 119, 135, 141, 152

Davidson College, 55-56, 121, 128, 130
Davis, Jefferson, 109, 110, 132
Dixie, 96
Douglas, Henry Kyd, 84, 85, 89, 98, 109; on TJJ's awkwardness, 20; on A.P.Hill, 90; on danger, 92; on TJJ's sense of humor, 98; on drinking, 101, 119-120, 126, 152
Emma, (slave in the Jackson's household), 62-63
Episcopal Church in Lexington, 130
Ewell, Richard, S., (Confederate general), 86, 99, 120, 151
Fairfax, 75
Fancy, see Little Sorrel
First Virginia Cavalry, 131
Fishburne, Clem, 55
Foot Cavalry, 84
Fort Hamilton, 3, 29, 34, 114, 140
Fort Lafayette, 35
Fort Meade, 36-39, 114
Franklin Society, 42, 43, 115, 141
Fredericksburg, 79, 109
Fremont, John Charles, (Union general), 85
French, William H., 36; his dispute with TJJ, 37-39, 120
Front Royal, (battle), 116
Fry, Birkett D., 12
Garnett, Richard Brooke, (Confederate general), 89, 149
George, (slave in the Jackson's household), 62
Gordonsville, 79
Governor's Island, 35
Graham, Dr. Archibald, 60, 143
Graham, James A. (Rev. and family), 77-78, 95
Grant, U.S., on TJJ's hypochondria, 31, 137
Guinea Station, 79, 105, 109
Hamilton's Crossing, 79
Harman, John, 83, 99
Harper's Ferry, 72, 115, 116
Harris, Caroline, 19
Hays, Peregrine, 136
Hays, Samuel L., (Congressman), 7-8

Henry, G.A., (Senator), 110
Hetty, (slave in the Jackson's household), 62, 63, 79, 143, 144
Hill, Ambrose Powell, (Confederate general), with TJJ at West Point, 12; conflict with TJJ, 89-90, 150; at Chancellorsville, 103-104, 120, 138, 140, 150, 151, 153
Hill, Daniel Harvey, (Confederate general), meets TJJ, 22; at Chapultepec, 25; on TJJ's early religious beliefs, 27; on TJJ in Florida, 39; in Lexington, 40-41, 47; helps TJJ to join church, 49; introduces TJJ to Miss Junkin, 51; leaves Lexington, 55; on TJJ's nervousness, 60, 92; on the name Stonewall, 71-72; death of a son, 77; on TJJ and danger, 92; 121, 129, 130, 151
Hill, Isabella, (Mrs. D.H., nee Morrison), 47, 52, 55, 56, 121, 129
Hood, John B. (Confederate general), 84
Hooker, Joseph, (Union general), 81; at Chancellorsville, 102, 131, 147
Hot Springs, 30, 59
Imboden, John D., 100, 122, 151, 152
Irisarri, Archbishop of Mexico, 27
Irwin, Harriet, (nee Morrison, TJJ's sister-in-law), 78, 129, 146
Jackson, Andrew, 15
Jackson, Cummins, (TJJ's uncle), 2-3; death, 3; 5, helps TJJ to go to West Point, 7; 61, 122, 123, 135, 136, 137, 143
Jackson, Elinor, (nee Junkin - TJJ's first wife), meets TJJ, 51; death, 52, 55, 58, 78, 110, 115, 125, 141
Jackson, Elizabeth, (TJJ's sister), 1, 123, 141
Jackson, Elizabeth Brake, (Mrs. Edward, TJJ's stepgrandmother), 2, 114, 118, 122-123, 135
Jackson family, 1-2, 8-9, 122
Jackson House, (in Lexington, VA), 5, 56, 65, 112, 115, 124, 143
Jackson, John G., 9, 123

INDEX

Jackson, Jonathan, (TJJ's father), 1-2, financial difficulties, 9; TJJ's middle name, 9-10, 114, 123, 135, 136

Jackson, Julia, (TJJ's daughter), 77-81, 106, 113, 116; 146

Jackson, Julia Neale, later Woodson, (TJJ's mother), 1-2, 9, 78, 114, 123-124, 136

Jackson, Laura, see Arnold

Jackson, Mary Anna, (nee Morrison - TJJ's second wife) on TJJ's intellect, 14; on TJJ in Florida, 39; 42, on TJJ's social skills, 47; with ladies, 48; corresponds with TJJ, 50; meets TJJ, 51; wooed by TJJ, 55; life in Lexington, 56-58; honeymoon, 59; at a spa, 60; her slaves, 62; housekeeping, 62; her dowry, 65; furnishing house, 66; on Little Sorrel, 73; as war starts, 74; visits TJJ at Manassas, 75-76; in Winchester, 76; birth of child, 78; visits TJJ with the baby, 79-81; 85, sings Dixie, 96; 102, at TJJ's deathbed, 106; at funeral, 109; as a widow, 112-113, dies, 113; 115, 117, 142, 143, 144, 146, 150

Jackson, Mary Graham, (TJJ's daughter), 77, 115

Jackson Mill, 2-3, 5, 6, 19, 61, 123, 135

Jackson, Thomas Jonathan, birth, 1; youthful fisherman, 4; early education, 5, 136; adventure on the Mississippi, 5, 136; first jobs, 6; applies to West Point, 7; ancestors, 8-9; feelings about his father, 9; acquires middle name, 9-10; studies at West Point, 11-15; plodding scholar, 14, 137; academic standing at West Point, 15; vacation misadventure, 19; in Mexican War, 21-28; studies Spanish, 24, 27; distinguishes himself in battles in Mexico, 24-26; visits sister in Beverly, 30; stuck in a persimmon tree, 32; at Fort Meade, 36-39; conflict with Maj. French, 78-39; accepts position at VMI, 39; as teacher at VMI, 41, 88, 141; his memory, 42; public speaking, 42, 141; his students' opinion of him, 44; habit of falling asleep, 48, 85; first marriage 51-52; European travels, 54-55; second marriage, 56, 142; buys a house, 56; adult study habits, 57; visits spas, 59-60; gardening, 61, 63; teaches Sunday school, 63; on slavery, 61-63, 64; becomes bank director, 65; furnishing his house, 66, 144; feelings about the Union, 68; leaves for the war, 69; "Who is is this Major Jackson?", 70; earns the name Stonewall, 71; gets Little Sorrel, 72; gets command of the Valley of Virginia, 76; meets his daughter, 80; as a military leader, 83; his military strategy, 84; called Wagon Hunter, 87; demanding court martials, 88; tries to resign command, 91; picking blackberries, 92; as music lover, 95-96, Maryland campaign, 101; wounded at Chancellorsville, 103, 147; his dying words, 107; funeral in Lexington, 110; his library, 144

Jackson and alcohol, a youthful revel, 18; 100; "I fear it more than Yankee bullets," 101; 104, 152

Jackson and ladies, 19-20, dancing, 20, 35; Mexican senoritas, 24, 28; in Lexington, 48; his female admirers 95-96, 138

Jackson and money, as a young officer, 27-28; his earnings, 64; family finances, 65; spending habits, 66; 136, 144

Jackson and slavery, in youth 61; family servants, 62; Mary Anna's slaves, 62; starts Colored Sunday School, 63; works alongside servants, 63; his views, 63-64; 65, 143, 144

Jackson's arm, 104, 125

Jackson's character, youthful ambitions 7; maxims, 17; lack of mercy, 17; disregards danger, 25, 93; tells a lie, 25; "You may be whatever you resolve to be," 16, 42; obeying orders, 43, 89; "He is as systematic as a multiplication table...", 44; passion for truth, 47-48; "I have no gift for seeming," 48; punctuality, 57, 69; on military duty, 74, 79; secrecy, 79, 83-84; on child rearing, 80; military philosophy, 82-85; never calls a council of war, 83; refuses to compromise, 88-89; conflicts with fellow officers, 89; dirty rifle incident, 88, 149; ambitious, 90, 150, 152, loves danger, 92-93, 151; modest man, 97; sense of humor, 97-98; on profanity, 99; clear mind to meet death, 105, 138, 140, 141

Jackson's children, 77-78, 138, see also Julia Jackson, and Mary Graham Jackson

Jackson's fame, his photo, 81; how his men saw him, 82-83, 84; with press, 94; with ladies, 95-96; receives gifts, 95-97; with British reporters, 97

Jackson's health, early complaints, 31; advice of physician, 32; sucks on a lemon, 32; eye problems, 33; during Civil War, 33; wounded at first Manassas, 34; lifts arm above his head, 33; his diets, 34; during conflict with Maj. French, 38; keeping his alimentary canal straight, 47; daily regime, 57; in Lexington, 58; visits spas, 59, 115, 140; tonsils treated, 60; health diets, 60, 140; sleep habits, 35, 48, 85; during Civil War, 86; wounded at Chancellorsville, 103; arm amputated and last illness, 104-106; 139, 140

Jackson's horsemanship, as youth 3; at West Point, 19; in Mexico, 27;
Little Sorrel, 72; 80, 86, thrown off a horse in Maryland, 101; 136

Jackson's military promotions, brevet second lieutenant, 17; second lieutenant, 23; breveted captain, 24; breveted major, 25; colonel, 70; brigadier general, 90-91; major general, 76, 91; lieutenant general, 92

Jackson's military strategy, in Mexico, 25; 83-85; foot cavalry, 84

Jackson's nicknames, 15, 43, 44, Stonewall, 71; 145; 95, 97, 99, 118, 151

Jackson's religious life, in Mexico, 27; baptism, 29-30; tolerance, 30, 49, 139; leads prayers, 42; joins church, 49; observance of Sabbath, 50, 148; daily prayers, 58; with Negroes, 61, 63; tithes, 66; military, 69; in Winchester, 77; daughter baptized, 80; fighting on Sabbath, 86, 148; trust in God, 86; capital punishment, 89; about death, 93, 104; "I had always wanted to die on Sunday," 106; at West Point, 138; 139, 150

Jackson's social life, at West Point, 14; with girls, 19-20; dancing, 20, 49; in Mexico, 24, 27; at Fort Hamilton, 34-35; playing cards, 35, 140; in Lexington, 47-49, 61; with children, 77; with his staff, 86; during Civil War, 95-96, 98

Jackson, Warren, (TJJ's brother), 2, raft adventure 5; 125, 135, 136

Jalapa, 23

James River, 110

Jim (TJJ's servant), see Lewis

Johnston, Joseph E. (Confederate general), 148

Junkin, Eleanor, (TJJ's first wife), see Jackson

Junkin, George, Rev. Dr., (TJJ's father-in-law), 52, 69, 125

Junkin, Julia Rush, (TJJ's mother-in-law), 52, 125

INDEX

Junkin, Maggie, see Preston
Junkin, W.F., Rev., (TJJ's brother-in-law), 110
Kernstown, (battle), 116, 149
Kester, Conrad, buys fish, 4
Lacey, Beverly Tucker, (TJJ's military chaplain), 80, 81, 105, 108, 125
Lacey, Drury (Rev.), 56
Lee, Robert E., (Confederate general), 3, 72, 86; in A.P.Hill case, 90; on TJJ, 92; on profanity, 99; on loss of TJJ, 105, 108, 125, 130, 147, 151, 153
Leigh, Benjamin, Watkins (Capt.), 103, 153
Letcher, John, (and wife), 109-110
Lewis County, 6, 114
Lewis, Jim, 86, 97, 109, 126
Lexington, 33, 40, 46-48, 49, 51, 52, 54-59, 62, 65-66, 69, 73, 75, 81, 108, 109, 110, 114, 126, 131
Lightburn, Joe, 5-6, 61
Lincoln, Abraham, 145
Little Sorrel, 72-73, 101, 103, 109, 127
Longstreet, James, (Confederate general), 92
Loring, William W., (Confederate general), 91, 150
Lyle, John Blair, 49
Lynchburg, 109-110
Magruder, John Bankhead, 24; at Chapultepec, 25; 28, 127
Manassas, first battle, 33, 34, 66, 71, 75, 91, 99, 115, 118, 131, 147-148
Manassas, second battle, 84, 100, 116, 120, 132, 150
Marshall, (packet boat), 110
Martinsburg, moving railroad cars, 87
Maryland campaign, 101
Mason, Clairborne, 87, 148-149
Maury, Dabney, as cadet at West Point, 12-14; TJJ's drunken frolic, 18; on TJJ's horsemanship, 19; in Mexico, 22; on TJJ's health problems, 33; on TJJ's teaching, 44; on TJJ's feuds, 89, 128; 137, 140, 141, 149
McCally, James, (Dr.), 1

McClellan, George B., (Union general), at West Point, 14, 137, 140
McDowell, (battle), 116
McDowell, Irvin, (Union general), 71, 148
McGuire, Hunter H. (Dr.), at first Manassas, 34; 90, 98, at Chancellorsville, 104-106, 109, 128
Mexican War, (1846-1848), 21-28
Mexico City, 23, 24, 25, 26, 27
Military uniforms during Civil War, 70-71
Mississippi River, youthful adventure, 5
Monongahela River, 4
Monterey, 21, 23, 114
Morrison, Eugenia, (TJJ's sister-in-law), 51, 55, 129
Morrison family, 128-129
Morrison, Joseph, (TJJ's aide), 81; on TJJ's staff, 85; 105, 129, 153
Morrison, Mary Anna, see Jackson
Morrison, Robert, (Rev. Dr., TJJ's father-in-law), 55-56; on slaves, 65, 129
Moss Neck, 34, 78, 116
New York City, 32, 54, 55, 56, 60, 66, 101
Niagara Falls, 52, 56
North River, (now Maury), 110
Northampton, 60
Old Baldy, 120
Palmer, John Williamson, 147
Parkersburg, 123
Pendleton, Sandie, (TJJ's aide), 104-105, 108, 110, 126, 130, 146
Pendleton, William N., (Rev.), 130
Philadelphia, 66
Pickett, George (Confederate general), 138
Pope, John, (Union General), 100, 116
Port Republic, (battle), 85, 116
Presbyterian Church in Lexington, 49, 51, 114, 132, 140
Preston, J.T.L., 53, 98, 118, 125, 131, 142

Preston, Margaret Junkin, (sister-in-law), 51-53, 98, on TJJ's habits, 57, on TJJ humor, 97; 118, 125, 131, 141, 142, 143
Ramsey, Rev. 110
Richmond, 69-70, 76, 81, 85, 91, 104, 109, 113, 116, 147
Rockbridge Artillery, 70, 130
Rockbridge Baths, 59
Rodes, Robert E. (Confederate general), 153
Romney expedition, 100, 116
Salem College, 122, 129
Santa Anna, Antonio Lopez de, 24
Scott, Winfield, (Gen.), 23, singles TJJ out, 26; reprimands TJJ, 39
Seminole wars, 36-37, 121, 127
Seven Days battles, 34, 116, 127, 132
Sharpsburg, see Antietam
Shields, James, (Union general), 86
Smith, Francis Henney, (Superintendent of VMI), 40, 43, defends TJJ, 89, 141
Smith, James Power, (Capt.), 105, 109, 110, 153
Spencer, John C., (Secretary of War), 8
Stonewall, source of TJJ's nickname, 71, 117-118, 145
Stonewall Brigade, 45, 78, 110, 150, 153
Stonewall Jackson Hospital, 124
Stuart, J.E.B., (Confederate general), 3, 81, presents TJJ with a coat, 96-97; their friendship, 98-99; at Chancellorsville, 104, 108; 131-132, 153
Talbot, John, (Col.), fish story, 4
Taliaferro, William B., (Confederate general), 83, 87, 132, 151
Tampa, 36, 38
Taylor, Francis, 21, 28, introduces TJJ to religion, 29
Taylor, George, 22
Taylor, Richard, (Confederate general), 88; on TJJ's ambition, 90, 132
Taylor, Zachary, 21, 72, 132

United Daughters of Confederacy, 124
Valley Campaign, 17, 72, 85, 92
Vera Cruz, (battle), 23, 114
Virginia Literary Fund, 6
Virginia Military Institute, (VMI), 37, 38, 40-41, 44, 46, 56, 57, 60, 64, 69, cadets leave for Richmond, 69; museum, 73; 88, 98, 110, 114, 129, 131, 136, 144
Wagon Hunter, 87
Walker, James A., 44-45, 114
War casualties, 111
Warm Springs, 59
Washington, DC, 8, 18, 30, 83
Washington College, 40, 46, 47, 51, 69, 121, 122, 125, 126
Washington, George, 126
West Fork River, 4
West Point, 7, 8, 11-15, 18, 21, 22, 31, 37, 41, 44, 66, 70, 88, 114, 117, 121, 125, 127, 128, 130, 131, 133, 137, 138, 140, 149
Weston, 2, 114
White Sulphur Springs, 59
White, Sylvanus, (TJJ's cousin), 13, 123
White, William Spotswood, (Rev.), 48, 50, 66, 69, 110, 132
Whiting, William, H.C., (Confederate general), 83, 133
Wilcox, Cadmus, 18, 138
Wilson, Clarendon J.L. (Dominie), 18, 138
Winchester, 76-78, 87, 91, 95, 96, 98, 101, 116, 128
Winder, C.S., (Confederate general), 89, 149
Wise, Henry A., (Confederate general), 99
Withers, Alexander, (Col.), 6, 63, 136
Woodson, Blake B., 2, 114, 124
Woodson, William Wirt, (TJJ's half brother), 65, 124, 133
Yerby, William, 80

ORDER FORM

Please send me _____ copies of

OLD JACK

$12.95 plus $3.50 shipping and handling for first book $2.00 shipping for each additional book.

(Discount on orders over 10 copies. Write for prices.)

NAME: _____

ADDRESS: _____

_____

_____

I enclose $ _____ (Check or Money Order)

      Mail to: **Cedar Hill Press**
                 1093 Forge Road
                 Lexington, VA 24450

13.99 - '06 (LEXINGTON, VA.)

CONTENTS

Introduction v

Chapter One:
Grace for Mistakes 1

Chapter Two:
Grace to Change 27

Chapter Three:
Grace to Reach the Lost 66

INTRODUCTION

I was born into a Christian home, so I've heard about grace all my life. Everyone talks about grace ... but sometimes we don't really understand it. What is perhaps the most well-known of all Christian songs?

"AMAZING GRACE"

*"Amazing grace, how sweet the sound,
That saved a wretch like me.
I once was lost, but now I'm found;
Was blind, but now I see."*

Grace is a very "Christianese" term that is often misunderstood by both Christians and nonbelievers. When you break it down, it is a simple concept that has daily application in our lives. The definition most often given to grace is: a God-given opportunity to change with His power. That sounds Christianese too, doesn't it? But that really does say it all. Grace is a gift of God, and there's absolutely nothing we can do (or have done) to persuade Him to give it to us — He gives His grace because He chooses to.

One of the more frequently asked questions by non-believers (and some believers too) is: "If God is a good God, then why is there so much bad stuff happening in the world?" God gets blamed for a lot of things: war, sickness, death, disaster. But a great modern-day preacher once said, "If God's grace and goodness were not being manifested in our world, this place would be hell!"

The Bible tells us that God's goodness is absolute, and it is revealed in His mercy and grace, demonstrated through His

Introduction

long-suffering, and seen in His benevolence and care. God's grace is His gift — and He gives it to us daily, although often we don't even recognize it.

FAITH-SHAKERS

All of us have challenges in our lives, and all of us (myself included) need God's grace to help us through. None of us are exempt from the day-to-day problems of life, and all of us receive (whether we acknowledge it or not) God's grace to see us through those troubles. Let's look at some common things that shake our faith and then learn how God's grace can help us through them.

Do you ever struggle with fear? One time, when we were ministering in Pakistan, the crowds were so big and so aggressive that I was shaking like a leaf, especially on the last night. One of our ministry helpers, Toby, reassured us, "You all will be out of here in a minute" — because the look on my face probably said everything. Later, one of our video technicians remarked that on the video tapes, I looked terrified! I was shaking so hard and just praying in tongues because I was so scared. Maybe you've never wrestled with fear like that, but I have.

Do you struggle with people? Some people come into our lives and rub us the wrong way. Sometimes we don't want to be around people. Sometimes we're co-dependent with people. Struggling with people is one of the biggest faith-shakers we'll encounter.

Another common problem is insecurity. A lot of troubles in our world are because of a lack of self-confidence. When people who suffer from insecurity start putting other people in jeopardy to satisfy their own inner longings for security, that has a "domino" effect. And uncertainty goes right along with insecurity. We just can't seem to make a good decision; we're not certain of ourselves — that's uncertainty.

Then there's "getting what I deserve." I had a friend whose mother died of cancer — a brutal death, absolutely gruesome and gory — and she wasn't even 50 years old. I remember saying, "God, of all people, she deserved to be healed." Have you ever said something like that to God, maybe in the back of your head? Sometimes we think we deserve more than we're getting.

Sometimes we wrestle with a lack of faith. "Oh, I can't ... that's too hard. That's too big for me to believe for." Christians — who base their entire lives on faith — are sometimes the worst doubters around! We forget that first simple act of faith that brought us into the kingdom of God. We are infected by "rationality" and "intellectualism" and other mind games that erode our sense of childlike faith. We forget our true perspective: we are children and God is our Father — and He is a whole lot bigger and stronger and wiser than we are!

How about "telling God what to do"? Have you ever thought, *God, you need to do this, this, and this?* We give Him our "job description." That's probably not a good idea.

I know we've all wrestled with pride. James 4:6 reads: *"God is opposed to the proud, but gives grace to the humble."* That's one of those verses that really impacts us. We are born with pride, and learning to be humble is hard work.

Sometimes our flesh is the struggle. Our rollercoaster emotions, our stubborn wills, our "creature comforts" — these are the things that make up our "flesh." We want to be strong in God, but our flesh — our human weakness — seems to always undermine what we want to do.

Some of us have wrestled with violence. It's been a hard thing for us to control our impulses and not just strike out at others, sometimes with forceful behavior, violence, and/or words. Matthew 5:38–39 says, *"You have heard that it was said, 'Eye for eye, and tooth for tooth.' But I say to you, do not show opposition against an evil person; but whoever slaps you on your right cheek, turn the other toward him also."* That's sometimes very tough to do!

Failure can be a big, big problem. We've heard the saying, "If at first you don't succeed, try, try again. But few of us are willing to risk ourselves again if we mess up the first time. Embarrassment, loss of pride, loss of self-esteem — these are all things that can happen if we don't receive grace in our times of failure. They can totally defeat us for our entire life.

Maybe another problem we've been shaken by is backsliding. For a short time in my life, I didn't really believe in Jesus. But as I worked through some issues,

I made a fresh commitment to Him. It had so hurt my heart that I had turned my back on Him! And it really rocked me that He would have the grace to take me back.

These are some of the things that I wrestle with — some faith-shakers. You probably have your own list of faith-shakers. But I want to encourage you: there is grace for these areas! One thing we need to be aware of is that grace isn't just there to get us through some problems. Sometimes we think, *God, just give me grace, and I'll make it through this.* But that's not the only purpose for grace.

THE TRAFFIC TICKET

Several years ago, I got a traffic ticket for rolling through a stop sign. I'm not a big traffic ticket person — hadn't had one in years. One day, I rolled through this stop sign. I paused and sort of slid past the stop sign — and then I got caught by a police officer.

I was guilty, and I admitted it. The police officer wrote out the ticket and said, "Now, because you rolled through the stop sign, you will have four points posted against your driver's license." (This would cause my car insurance to become more expensive.) "... and a $60 fine. You can just mail in your fine, or you can go to Traffic Court and try to get it reduced or dismissed."

I thought the four-point penalty on my license and the $60 fine were way too stiff. So of course, I decided, "Well, I'll just go to the Traffic Court and try to plea bargain it lower." When the date came, I went to court. I was sitting there doing all the right stuff, and before the court session was convened, I went to see the assistant district attorney in her office.

The assistant D.A. looked at my case and said to me, "So, you have a citation for rolling through a stop sign."

I answered, "Yes."

She asked, "Did you do it?"

"I did," I replied.

"Okay, here's what I'm willing to offer you," she responded. "I'll cut the points down to two, and you'll still pay a $60 fine."

I cheekily protested, "What do you mean, two points? Is it still going to be a moving violation?"

"Yes, I can't change that."

"So why bother?" I retorted. "It's still going to be more money on my insurance. My driver's insurance is going to go up, and I still have to pay sixty dollars! So what difference does it make if you give me a four-point ticket or a two-point ticket? Who cares?" I'm honest. That's exactly what I said, and pretty much in a belligerent tone of voice.

She looked at me and she asked, "Are you guilty?"

I answered again, "Yes."

She finished, "Then take the two points and get out of here!"

I was so angry! I really needed grace, but I didn't get any — at least, I didn't get as much as I thought I needed.

Eventually, I was called before the very intimidating judge. I wasn't going to say anything to the judge because I was really nervous. But as I was standing before the judge, God started to deal with me: "Sarah, you did get grace. You just didn't appreciate what you got."

WHY GRACE?

Grace has three parts:
1. To get us through
2. To change us
3. To reach others

Grace is never meant to just get us slipping our way through something. Grace is meant to change us. It's not there to leave us the same as before. When we come through something by God's grace, we should be different than when we started. Then grace enables us to reach others. So, in this book, we're going to see how grace works and how it helps us in our weakness.

Chapter One

GRACE FOR MISTAKES

After you have suffered for a little while, the God of all grace, who called you to His eternal glory in Christ, will Himself perfect, confirm, strengthen, and establish you. (**1 PETER 5:10**)

"The God of all grace." There is no grace outside of God. If we think that we're giving grace that originated with us, we're deceiving ourselves. The grace that we give is the grace that we received. When we get grace, it's the God of all grace who gave it to us in the first place.

Look at 1 Peter 5:10 again: *"After you have suffered for a little while, the God of all grace, who called you to His eternal glory in Christ, will Himself perfect, confirm, strengthen, and establish you."* The God of all grace will perfect, confirm, strengthen, and establish us. The God of all grace will make us strong, firm, and steadfast! The God of all grace will help us where we are weak, where we fail, and in our shortcomings.

As I began to realize this, it so touched me. It was as though God took a picture of my insides and saw my mistakes and shortcomings. And I knew that if He could help me with this and bring me through — even as He brought Peter through — then He could bring you through too!

Those "faith-shakers" in the introduction actually came from the life of Simon

Peter, Peter the Rock, the fisherman, the Apostle. When we read about Peter, we mostly see his flaws and faults. We don't see the "final product" that Jesus saw: a person who would be a major founder of the early church. Often, we see Peter as a loud-mouthed, rash, ignorant fisherman who got into lots of trouble before he accomplished great things for God.

Isn't that the way we usually view ourselves? We are so convinced that we can't do anything because all we see are our problem areas. Thank God, He sees us as His precious children, with all our sins covered by the blood of the Lamb.

Peter was an awesome guy — which is good because the guy was a total walking mistake in many ways! He was constantly saying the wrong thing and misbehaving. One of the first times we meet him in the Bible, he was even doing the wrong thing.

FIRST MISTAKE: INSECURITY

In Luke 5, we read about one of Peter's first encounters with Jesus. It was in the morning. Peter and his fishing partners had just finished fishing and were mending their nets. (By the way, his real name was "Simon Bar-Jonah," but later, Jesus re-named him "Peter," which means "rock.") Jesus came along, borrowed Peter's boat, went out and preached a sermon, then came and gave the boat back to Peter. Then He said, "Simon, if you'll put your nets out (go out fishing again), you'll get a large harvest."

Peter said to Him, "I'm tired; we've been up all night, and we haven't caught a thing. But because you said to do it, I'll do it." So, what happened? He put his net out and had a huge, huge harvest!

Here's where Peter's first mistake took place: when they got the harvest, he rowed back to the shore, but instead of saying, "Thank you," he did something else.

Grace for Mistakes

Gratitude wasn't Peter's first response. He said to Jesus, "Get away from me! I'm a sinful man!" He pushed Him away! That's obviously a clear mistake. Peter was not grateful — he was fearful and insecure.

Jesus then answered, "No, no, no, I've got a plan for you. I'm going to make you a fisher of men." Even in his first encounter with Jesus, Peter messed up.

In John 21, when Peter realized it was Jesus Christ calling from shore, Peter didn't wait for the others to row the boat to shore but just jumped in and started swimming back to Jesus. He was so convinced that Jesus loved him that he wanted to reach Him immediately. That's what the grace factor does for you!

Later in John 21, we read where Jesus and Peter reconciled. This was after Jesus had been crucified, died, and resurrected, and He came to meet His disciples while they were fishing in Galilee. Jesus gave Peter the opportunity to affirm his love for Him. It was an awesome moment, and Jesus gave Peter grace and forgiveness he never forgot. Peter embraced Jesus rather than rejecting Him, and it changed his life forever.

That was what Jesus did for Peter and what Jesus does for us — although we may momentarily reject Him, He still reaches out and embraces us by His grace.

SECOND MISTAKE: FEAR

Peter's next mistake is found in Matthew 14. Jesus had sent the disciples on ahead in the boat, while He stayed to send the crowd of people away. Then He was alone on the mountainside, doing what He loved to do best: praying to (talking with) His Father.

In the meantime, the disciples got themselves into trouble. Isn't that just like us? We wander away from the presence of God, and trouble starts happening! So, the disciples were caught up in a huge storm.

They were in a little boat; the waves were crashing over them, and they were certain they were going to drown.

Jesus had to rescue them. The way He chose to come to them was remarkable: He just started walking across the water. Of course, it was dangerous to be out on the water in that storm. But did a storm like that stop Jesus? No! He just walked right over the whole problem — as calmly as if He were Master of the Universe. Which, of course, He is.

This feat impressed Peter so much that he forgot all about the storm and all about their future as fish food. Instead, Peter started looking at Jesus walking on the water, and he said, "That's really cool! I'd love to do that too! Can I come?"

Jesus answered, "Come on out!" So Peter started to walk out on the water, going straight for Jesus. At first, it was really neat. Peter was more afraid of losing Jesus or missing Him than he was of drowning. But then he looked away from Jesus — just for a second — and he saw the wind and waves, he started to sink. Peter's second mistake was taking his eyes off Jesus.

THIRD MISTAKE: NERVOUS CHATTER

The next mistake took place on the Mount of Transfiguration, and we read about it in Mark 9. Jesus went first, and then He was joined by Moses and Elijah. They were all up there, and they were glowing, radiant. Peter was afraid. He didn't know what to do, so he just started to chatter.

When some people get nervous, if they get a little afraid, they start to talk, talk, talk! Peter was so afraid and so nervous that he talked too much. That's another one of his shortcomings.

If you go back to John 21, when the disciples were talking with "the stranger on the shore," you'll see that the Bible says:

"None of the disciples ventured to inquire of Him, 'Who are You?' knowing that it was the Lord" (John 21:12). This included Peter — the guy who was always talking! Now, because of the grace factor, Peter had self-control. The grace of Jesus will take care of our mouths.

FOURTH MISTAKE: PRIDE

The next mistake on our list is pride. Let's look at it in Matthew 18:21–22:

> *Then Peter came up and said to Him, "Lord, how many times shall my brother sin against me and I still forgive him? Up to seven times?" Jesus said to him, "I do not say to you, up to seven times, but up to seventy-seven times."*

Peter thought he was being really cool, really magnanimous, really generous:

"Lord, how many times should I forgive someone, up to seven?" Jesus answered, "No, actually, limitless times."

Peter constantly had that "foot-in-mouth" syndrome. We all have pride, we all have fear. Maybe when we're afraid, we talk too much. Maybe when things go poorly all around us, our faith wavers and we begin to sink. Maybe when we get a miraculous thing from God — a great harvest — instead of saying, "Thank you," we avoid Him and say, "Ah, I'm not worthy. Get away from me!" We all have failures. We all make mistakes, and we need to face the grace. Because when we face the grace, there's change through grace.

Looking again at John 21, we see the risen Savior, Jesus, making breakfast for His disciples on the shore. They'd been out fishing all night, and they were tired and hungry. When He called to them in their boat, they came back to the shore and sat down to eat with Him. *"Jesus came and took the bread and gave it to them, and the fish likewise"* (John 21:13).

The interesting thing about this breakfast was that the disciples didn't actually earn any of it. They got more than they deserved. With Jesus, we always get more than we deserve — we get forgiveness that is limitless.

FIFTH MISTAKE: REBUKE

In Mark 14:27, during the Last Supper in the upper room in Jerusalem, on the eve of Passover, Jesus said to all His disciples, "You will all fall away."

Peter boasted, "Not me. Lord! Even if everybody else denies you, I'll never deny you!" He was so arrogant. "I can handle it. I won't deny you."

Jesus disagreed with him: "Yes, you will. Before the rooster crows three times, you're going to deny me."

"I'll even die for you, Jesus!" Peter was so prideful. He needed to face the grace because these were areas where there were clear shortcomings in his life.

In Matthew 16, Jesus told the disciples, "I'm going to the cross. I'm going to suffer. I'm going to go through a hard time."

Anyone who cares about another would do their best to help minimize problems, avoid trouble, and prevent disaster from overtaking their friend. I think that's what Peter was trying to do here. He rebuked Jesus by saying, "That'll never happen to you, Jesus. I'm going to keep you from doing that!"

Peter didn't realize there was a "bigger picture" that he just couldn't see. He couldn't see what God's eternal plan for Jesus really was. By rebuking Jesus and trying to interfere with Jesus's destiny, he was actually getting in God's way!

It was Jesus's destiny to die — after all, Jesus was *"the Lamb of God who takes away the sin of the world"* (John 1:29). By rebuking Jesus, Peter was trying to keep Him from His destiny.

Now watch this: because it was Jesus's destiny to go to the cross, He also had a destiny for Peter. Peter's destiny was not to fish for fish, but to be a fisher of men. Notice what Jesus said to Peter in John 21: "Peter, do you love me? Feed my lambs." He was saying, "Peter, be a fisher of men. Don't miss your destiny; fish for souls!" It was the grace to fulfill his destiny.

God has a plan and a destiny for each one of us. But without grace to change us, we will never make our destiny. Ever. We'll be failures, insecure, always falling short. We need the grace factor!

SIXTH MISTAKE: WEAK FLESH

Another of Peter's mistakes came in the garden of Gethsemane (Mark 14). This was a critical moment in Jesus's life — He was about to face His greatest trial ever — and Peter fell asleep. He was tired, but Jesus asked, "Can't you just pray?"

Mumbling, covering his failure to stay alert, Peter answered, "Oh yeah. Lord, we'll pray." Next thing we know, he was snoring again.

Then Jesus came, asking again, "Can't you just pray?" Don't you think Jesus needed His friends for reinforcement? But where were they? Asleep.

"Okay, okay! We're praying, Lord." But Peter still fell back to sleep. Even at a critical time, he was still failing.

Sometimes we feel that way. We feel like we go from one mistake — one failure after another — to another. But there's grace and hope for us! We're not failures, not walking mistakes! There's grace, hope, and change for us!

Notice the setting in John 21. It was in the morning, after the disciples had been fishing all night long. They'd had a hard night, hard work, but there had been no fruit. Now look at what Peter did this time.

He didn't just ignore Jesus and say, "Oh, that's you over there? Okay, you can just wait for a little bit; just hold on. I'm kind of tired, too tired to get over to you." Peter didn't do that this time. He didn't surrender to his flesh. Now, because of the grace in his life, his strong spirit overcame his flesh! He said, "No matter what it takes, I'm going to get to Jesus. I don't care if I'm tired; I don't care if there's an ocean in front of me. I don't care what it takes — I'm going to get to Jesus!"

His flesh no longer dominated or dictated. Rather, grace had changed him. The grace factor totally undercuts and undermines weak flesh.

SEVENTH MISTAKE: VIOLENCE

Peter is one of the most clearly described people in the Bible. His heart is so clearly revealed to us that it seems as though we know him well. So, what's the next thing we learn about Peter? He was an impulsive, violent kind of person.

John 18 gives us a detailed account. Here we find Peter doing what he did best: overreacting, behaving impulsively. He was rudely awakened from a much-disturbed sleep by the sudden arrival of Judas and the others, ready to arrest Jesus. As a response, his first instinct was to behave violently and cut off the ear of the high priest's servant! (v. 10). Would you say that he had a shortcoming in this area? He was cutting off ears! I would consider that a big mistake!

Fortunately for Malchus, the high priest's servant, Jesus the healer happened to be at the right place at the right time. In Luke 22:51, we're told that He touched the man's ear, and it was completely healed. Once again, Jesus was cleaning up after Peter's mistakes.

By the time Jesus was led away, Peter was not there right by his side, saying, "How can I help you, Lord?" Instead (maybe he was finally cautious for the first time in his life!), Peter was watching from a distance. He was sneaking up a little, watching to see how everything was going (Luke 22).

In John 21, Jesus talked about what kind of death Peter was going to experience:

> *"Truly, truly I tell you, when you were younger, you used to put on your belt and walk wherever you wanted; but when you grow old, you will stretch out your hands and someone else will*

put your belt on you, and bring you where you do not want to go." Now He said this, indicating by what kind of death he would glorify God. And when He had said this, He said to him, "Follow Me!" **(JOHN 21:18-19)**

Matthew 26:52 reads: *Then Jesus said to him, "Put your sword back into its place; for all those who take up the sword will perish by the sword."*

Historians say that Peter was crucified upside down. When he knew they were going to crucify him, he said, "Don't crucify me right side up. That's how my Lord died, and I don't deserve that. Crucify me upside down." Talk about a violent, brutal death — the grace embrace enabled him to go through that successfully.

The grace factor defeated the impulsive violence in Peter and turned him into a nonviolent person.

EIGHTH MISTAKE: DENIAL

Then, almost the last of Peter's mistakes, he denied Jesus. Peter had the opportunity to be with Jesus for two to three years and became close to Him, yet he was still making these kinds of mistakes. So, if Peter made them and he came through, how much more grace is there for us? We can come through!

Just because he denied Jesus didn't mean it was all over. People came up to Peter a couple of different times and insisted, "You are with that guy Jesus!"

"No, no. I'm not with Him! I'm not with Him!" Three times, he denied Jesus. Three times he said, "I don't know what you're talking about!" Right when he denied Him the third time, the rooster crowed (Luke 22:60).

The Bible then tells us that Jesus turned and looked at Peter. But in the Greek, it's not that He looked at him, it says that

He looked through him. Jesus will look through us, see our failures, but still love us and go to the cross for us. He'll look through us to the very heart of who we are and still go to the cross for us.

But then, on the shores of the sea of Galilee after His resurrection, Jesus asked Peter three times, "Do you love Me?"

> *Now when they had finished breakfast, Jesus said to Simon Peter, "Simon, son of John, do you love Me more than these?" He said to Him, "Yes, Lord; You know that I love You." He said to him, "Tend My lambs." He said to him again, a second time, "Simon, son of John, do you love Me?" He said to Him, "Yes, Lord; You know that I love You." He said to him, "Shepherd My sheep." He said to him the third time, "Simon, son of John, do you love Me?" Peter was hurt because*

He said to him the third time, "Do you love Me?" And he said to Him, "Lord, You know all things; You know that I love You." Jesus said to him, "Tend My sheep." (JOHN 21:15-17)

Jesus gave Peter the opportunity to change, to repent, and to undo what he had done before. Peter knew He wasn't asking him some idle, repetitious questions designed to embarrass him. Peter knew that Jesus was allowing him to erase the mistakes of his past. He was the same one who looked through Peter in the moment of Peter's greatest mistake and said, "You're still worth it to Me; I'll go to the cross for you."

"Do you love Me? I died for you. But Peter, do you love Me?" He asks us the same thing. "Do you love Me? Yes, you may have denied Me. Yes, you may have been afraid. Yes, you may have all of these faults, but do you love Me? Do you love Me?" Because if we love Him, He will give us the grace that changes us forever!

It was the touch of grace on Peter that enabled him to love Jesus, to embrace Him and say, "Yes, Lord, I love you." He didn't deny Jesus again after that.

In fact, he could not deny Jesus. An aspect of Peter that we read about in the book of Acts was his unswerving faith, his confidence, his belief, and his love for Jesus.

> *But Peter and John answered and said to them, "Whether it is right in the sight of God to listen to you rather than to God, make your own judgment; for we cannot stop speaking about what we have seen and heard." . . . But Peter and the apostles answered, "We must obey God rather than men."*
> **(ACTS 4:19-20; 5:29)**

The grace factor will help us, change us, and enable us to say wholeheartedly, "Yes, Lord, I love you!" Where we've been feeble and denied Jesus in the past, His grace will come along and help us. My challenge to you is: will you receive the grace He's offering?

NINTH MISTAKE: FAILURE

Finally, we see Peter's last mistake, his last shortcoming. Jesus had suffered on the cross; He died, and they put Him in the tomb. He rose from the dead, and what did Peter do?

After Jesus's death and resurrection, when He had already revealed Himself to His disciples several times, we didn't see Peter going out, winning the lost, preaching. Instead, Peter decided, "Forget it. I'm going back to fishing!" Not only did he go back to fishing, but he also took several of the other apostles with him. You talk about failure — the guy was a big-time failure!

Here's what Jesus said to him: "You're not a failure at all." In fact, Jesus said to him, *"Feed My sheep."* He wasn't telling Peter to do something he was not enabled to do. If He tells us to feed His sheep, He will enable us to do it. That's part of grace. If God asks you to do something, then God will shred the failure in your life and enable you — through His grace — to be successful.

Even in his failure, Jesus embraced him. Peter received it and came out better than when he started. Here's what Peter later wrote about that grace embrace in his own letter: *"After you have suffered for a little while, the God of all grace, who called you to His eternal glory in Christ, will Himself perfect, confirm, strengthen, and establish you"* (1 Peter 5:10).

By his own admission, the God of all grace visited Peter and touched him. Peter faced the grace... and was totally changed.

GRACE TO CHANGE

Second Corinthians 6:1 says, *"Working together with Him, we also urge you not to receive the grace of God in vain."* Grace is not just to pull us through, it's to change us! There are often times that we get grace in our life — maybe it's not in the way we want it, maybe it's not as much as we want — but the purpose of grace is to change us.

In all honesty, I have stopped rolling through stop signs (mostly). It's not because of the two-points, the four points, the fines, or whatever. I have stopped rolling through stop signs because the grace was there to change me — not to let me get through something, but to change me.

There are times when various things come along in our lives, and we have grace. It may not be in the form we would like or in the quantity we want, but it's still there. It's not just to let us squeak by with no punishment; rather, it's to change us. That's the purpose of grace.

Chapter Two

GRACE TO CHANGE

But by the grace of God I am what I am, and His grace toward me did not prove vain; but I labored even more than all of them, yet not I, but the grace of God with me. (1 CORINTHIANS 15:10)

The life of the apostle Paul was totally the result of God's grace! He knew where he had come from. Paul knew he was nobody special — in fact, he was a real terror to the Christians! But Paul's own testimony was: "God's grace wasn't without effect. It had a big effect on me."

The principle of God's grace is going to be very strategic for our lives. Sometimes people think of "grace" as just what you say over food: "Somebody say grace," and then we all eat. But that's not necessarily what grace is. Sometimes we think grace is what we've gotten away with. Somebody didn't catch us; we didn't get punishment. "I got grace!"

If we're really going to be serious about grace from God, it's beyond that. Let's look at grace in relationship to Paul. Paul is a phenomenal man who wrote about grace because he was a major recipient of it.

SAUL: BEFORE GRACE

First, we'll look at Paul in his pre-grace state. (If you want to call him Saul, that would be accurate as well.) As we already learned when studying the life of Simon Peter, when grace touches you, it changes you. When grace touched Saul, he wasn't

Saul anymore — he became Paul. (Interestingly enough, when grace touched Simon, he was changed into Peter.) When grace touches us, we are changed.

To see the change in Paul, let's look at what happened to him in his pre-grace state. If the man "Saul" walked into a church today, we'd all probably hit the ground or bolt out the doors because he was so violent. He persecuted Christians. He was religiously zealous for God, and he was very aggressive.

"I'll do whatever it takes to kill those Christians!" He was restless, looking everywhere, couldn't sit still long. He was cruel and vindictive:

> *Now Saul approved of putting Stephen to death. And on that day a great persecution began against the church in Jerusalem, and they were all scattered throughout the*

regions of Judea and Samaria, except for the apostles. Some devout men buried Stephen, and mourned loudly for him. But Saul began ravaging the church, entering house after house; and he would drag away men and women and put them in prison.
(ACTS 8:1-3)

Saul, still breathing threats and murder against the disciples of the Lord, went to the high priest, and asked letters from him to the synagogues of Damascus, so that if he found any who were of the Way, whether men or women, he might bring them bound to Jerusalem.
(ACTS 9:1-2)

"I am a Jew, born in Tarsus of Cilicia, but brought up in this city, educated under Gamaliel, strictly according to

the Law of our fathers, being zealous for God just as you all are today. I persecuted this Way to the death, binding and putting both men and women into prisons, as also the high priest and all the Council of the elders can testify. From them I also received letters to the brothers, and started off for Damascus in order to bring even those who were there to Jerusalem as prisoners to be punished."
(ACTS 22:3-5)

For you have heard of my former way of life in Judaism, how I used to persecute the church of God beyond measure and tried to destroy it; and I was advancing in Judaism beyond many of my contemporaries among my countrymen, being more extremely zealous for my ancestral traditions. **(GALATIANS 1:13-14)**

This was Saul before grace: cruel and vindictive. Remember when Stephen was being stoned by the crowd — who was standing by watching? It was Saul. It says he was there giving his approval. If we saw someone being beaten to death with rocks and stood there saying, "Yeah, hit him harder!" — isn't that cruel and vindictive? Absolutely. That was pre-grace Saul.

DAMASCUS ROAD GRACE

But here's what happened: Saul had a Damascus Road encounter, and it was Damascus Road grace. Acts 9:3–8 reveals:

> *Now as he was traveling, it happened that he was approaching Damascus, and suddenly a light from heaven flashed around him; and he fell to the ground and heard a voice saying to him, "Saul, Saul, why are you persecuting Me?" And he said, "Who*

are You, Lord?" And He said, "I am Jesus whom you are persecuting, but get up and enter the city, and it will be told to you what you must do." The men who traveled with him stood speechless, hearing the voice but seeing no one. Saul got up from the ground, and though his eyes were open, he could see nothing; and leading him by the hand, they brought him into Damascus.

This was a massive amount of grace which was given to Saul. What is "Damascus Road grace"? It is a very significant event that intersects the course of one's life, a junction in the road where one is confronted with a significant alternative to the present path. To keep it simple, we could easily say, "a turning point." Let me give you a personal example of my own Damascus Road experience.

The week before Reece and I were married, I was at home, having dinner with my parents. We were discussing the plans and schedule for the week in relation to the wedding on the following Saturday. In the middle of the discussion, my mother mentioned that she was going to attend a revival service at a different church in the city on Sunday night. I was very surprised at this because at that time, our church had Sunday night services, and something had to be very unusual for Mom not to attend our normal Sunday night service. She explained that there was an evangelist in town for the week, that he was being mightily used by God, and that the Holy Spirit was moving in powerful ways in these services.

At this time in my life, I was an extremely skeptical and analytical person and was trying to become even more scholarly and intellectual. As a result, I was fairly skeptical about the "move of God." While growing up, I had had some very powerful encounters with God that were extremely authentic and brought about some significant changes in my life. At this time, however, I had become very doubtful and was a borderline cynic.

I asked Mom to describe how she knew that this was an "authentic" move of God. While I listened, I wasn't really believing what she was saying. So, I asked if she thought I'd like these services. She firmly and quickly replied that she didn't think I'd like the services at all. I told her that I wanted to go and check out the service with her nonetheless, and she was fine with that.

When we attended the service that night, I listened politely but with skepticism. I heard nothing that would compromise the truth of God's Word. Then, as he was preaching, the evangelist walked by Mom and me ... and he touched me. I fell into

Mom's lap laughing — totally out of character for me.

Nevertheless, I knew that this was an authentic move of God, and I was hungry for more. I told Mom that I wanted to go back the next night, Monday. She was very surprised, but asked me to save her a seat because she would be late.

To this day, I am still uncertain as to what exactly happened to me other than the fact that I spent the bulk of the church service on the floor in front of everyone for two to three hours, being powerfully and radically touched by God, in a way similar to the experience the disciples had in Acts 2.

During that time, I really sensed God dealing with me about going into the ministry. I never wanted to be in the ministry. I had my own plans and aspirations, and I didn't want to "follow in anyone's footsteps." So, when God was dealing with me,

I was extremely serious with Him because I was familiar with some of the cost of being in the ministry.

When Mom arrived at the church from teaching her Bible school class at our church, she was looking for me to find her seat. Finally, she asked an usher if he knew whom and where I was. The usher explained that I had been on the floor under the power of God for the last two hours in the front of the auditorium. Needless to say, Mom was completely shocked.

From this experience — and several subsequent confirming encounters with God — I surrendered to God's will. Both my husband and I have entered the ministry. We continue to experience God's fullness in our lives in a multitude of ways.

That, for me, was "Damascus Road grace." You have probably had some similar things you'd consider huge encounters with God. That is God's grace.

Saul had a choice on that road. He made his choice when he got up. I made a choice when I got up. We all get grace, but the role it plays in our lives depends on what happens when we get up.

THE GIFT OF GRACE

Now imagine that I have just presented you with a beautifully wrapped package. "Wow, that's a cool gift!" you say, but you never open it. Or I give you a letter, but you never read it or never do anything about it. You will miss the whole point.

Some years ago, as the "Charismatic Renewal" movement was starting, people were being "slain in the Spirit" and falling on the floor. Always in the back of my mind, I thought, "But that's not the goal. The floor isn't the goal. The change is the goal." You can receive the grace but miss the point. That's not what grace is. Grace is for change.

All these experiences — Paul's, mine, and yours — are really grace opportunities. We've received a gift of grace.

SAUL BECAME PAUL

So, what did Saul do? When he got up off the Damascus Road, he couldn't see anything. He was blind for three days. He had changed and been altered. When we have a Damascus Road experience, when we receive grace, it's God saying, "Wait. Stop. You're going the wrong way. This is an opportunity for change." It's a paradigm shift. It's a change in the way we see things. When I got up off the floor at that church, the way I saw things was dramatically different. My husband will vouch for that. It was almost a 180-degree turn for me. I had been totally on my own, doing my own thing, and now, suddenly, I was doing something else.

That's what happened to Saul — who became Paul — a paradigm shift. Instead of beating people, stoning them, chasing them down to kill them — he was asking, "How can I help them?" That's a paradigm shift that comes from a touch of grace.

It was a large gift of grace that Saul got. That was a large gift of grace that I got. In our daily lives, every so often, we'll get a big gift of grace, but we also get some smaller ones, and sometimes we get some medium-sized ones. My goal is to help you recognize those gifts!

I would propose to you that every day we get a new gift of grace. Why do I say that? Well, read this:

> *The LORD's acts of mercy*
> *   indeed do not end,*
> *For His compassions do not fail.*

They are new every morning;
Great is Your faithfulness.
(LAMENTATIONS 3:22–23)

RECOGNIZING GRACE

Let's look at some examples of how to recognize grace. How about at work? Maybe you did something wrong, and instead of firing you, they just corrected you. That's grace. How about in school? You got a better grade than what you earned. I would call that grace. But it's grace with a purpose.

My husband had a friend in college who really had some academic struggles because engineering was a tough curriculum. A couple of his friends talked to the professors, saying, "Please give us grace. Please let us pass this class." Engineering classes are not simple.

There was one key guy who said, "Look, would you give me grace and let me pass this class so I can graduate?" The professor agreed, and the guy graduated and went on to do phenomenally huge things as an engineer. He's an awesome engineer now, but all of that came from that one gift of grace.

How about having a traffic ticket reduced or rescinded? I already told you about my experience with the traffic ticket. I really didn't think I deserved to get the ticket in the first place, so when I went to court, I protested it. Although the assistant district attorney agreed to reduce the ticket from four points to two points, I still thought I was being ripped off. I just couldn't recognize that I had been given a gift of grace! I thought I deserved more.

The whole time, God was speaking to me, "Sarah, you are getting grace. Keep your mouth shut and be glad for what you have." I didn't want to hear that. It took me awhile, but I finally realized that I had received a grace package, and then I was truly thankful for it.

GIFTS ARE FOR GIVING

When I left the traffic court and was finally in my car driving home, God spoke again: "You did get grace. You just didn't like the quantity of it. You just didn't like the quality of it." The whole point of that grace wasn't for me to get released from the ticket; the point of the grace was to change me! Consequently, I have stopped rolling through stop signs.

If you're driving behind me and my car stops totally, don't get frustrated and say, "Why doesn't she just move?" Instead, you'll know, "That's Sarah! She's coming to a full stop because she isn't going to let God's grace in her be without effect!" I would call this kind of grace behavioral grace — grace to change our behavior.

How about people? Have you ever had the experience where somebody likes you and you can't figure out why? "Wow, they think I'm pretty cool. I didn't give them anything. What's the deal?" Well, we're going to see how that's a gift of grace.

How about opportunities to do good to someone? When you're driving in rush-hour traffic and you're signaling to get over and people just get really close, cutting you off so you can't switch lanes? But then someone will extend grace and let you in. Well, it's not just for you to get in; it's also for you to give it back. That's "people grace" and "attitude grace."

How about grace with offerings? "Sarah, how can an offering be grace?" Well, that too is an opportunity for you to change your attitude. It's an opportunity for you to say, "God, thank you! I didn't really earn this — you gave it to me. Thank you, God, for the ability to work. Thank you for the talents. Thank you, Father!" This is an opportunity for us to show we're grateful. It's a chance for us to change from being stingy to being generous.

How about unexpected gifts? Sometimes we get a gift out of the blue. That's grace, and we have the opportunity to reciprocate.

How about special talents? Think about some of the talents we have. Those are packages of grace. Maybe we are really good with people and have excellent people skills. It's not just for our benefit; it's for the benefit of others, to reach and change others.

Maybe we have good administrative skills. Maybe we're good in an office — not everybody is! When we use our talents — either in our jobs, as volunteers, or even in full-time ministry — we need to use those skills to help others!

Think about the things you like to do, because those are usually your special talents. I like to teach. When I taught school, I was a very good schoolteacher! I loved it. The sad thing is, I used that talent for my own gratification. When my students would do well, I thought, *That's because I am so good.* I was not thanking God for His grace toward me or His gift to me of that talent. As a result, I would look to me, and the kids didn't get from God what they needed. Maybe you've received some packages of grace that you have mishandled too.

BEHAVIORAL GRACE

"Behavioral grace" means all those things we looked at earlier: getting a better grade than what we earned, getting a traffic ticket reduced, correction at work rather than getting fired. But the whole point of all of this isn't for us to say, "Wow! Check out this grace. I'm sure glad I didn't get fired!" or "Wow! I'm glad they reduced that ticket." All of that is excellent, but the whole point of the package isn't that we get away with it; the point is that we change.

Look at Romans: *"For sin shall not be master over you, for you are not under the Law but under grace. What then? Are we to sin because we are not under the Law but under grace? Far from it!"* (Romans 6:14–15).

Paul was saying, "Look, you got the grace. Does that mean you just keep sinning? If that were the case, you could be sinning all the more because you have abundant grace and can go out and do the same thing. Of course not; having grace means we don't keep on doing the same old thing. Grace changes us!"

The prayer of faith, which we pray when we accept God's gift of salvation is the most important prayer of our whole life. That prayer gives us eternal life. That prayer takes us into grace. Grace is not just unmerited favor; it's the unlimited supernatural ability of God to be poured out on those who love Him. God has grace to take us through this day and give us the victory.

GOD'S GRACE IN SPITE OF US

Sometimes we think we should always be "protected" by God's grace; that somehow, as Christians, we can always count on God's grace to prevent us from having problems or difficulties in our lives. That's not true. God's grace comes to us because He loves us, not because we deserve it. Paul wrote about this from his own experience.

"Are they Hebrews? So am I. Are they Israelites? So am I. Are they the seed of Abraham? So am I" (2 Corinthians 11:22). He is essentially saying, "According to the acceptable definition of the day, I was a perfect Jew, therefore I 'deserved' God's approval and protection."

What happened to Paul? Certainly not what anybody would consider to be obvious signs of God's approval!

Are they servants of Christ? — I am speaking as if insane — I more so; in far more labors, in far more imprisonments, beaten times without number, often in danger of death. Five times I received from the Jews thirty-nine lashes. Three times I was beaten with rods, once I was stoned, three times I was shipwrecked, a night and a day I have spent adrift at sea. I have been on frequent journeys, in dangers from rivers, dangers from robbers, dangers from my countrymen, dangers from the Gentiles, dangers in the city, dangers in the wilderness, dangers at sea, dangers among false brothers; I have been in labor and hardship, through many sleepless nights, in hunger and thirst, often without food, in cold and exposure. Apart from such external

things, there is the daily pressure on me of concern for all the churches.
(2 CORINTHIANS 11:23-28)

Paul went on to talk about his weaknesses, persecutions, the afflictions of Satan, and his "thorn in the flesh" (2 Corinthians 12:7) — and remember: all these things took place after he became a Christian! Yet Paul wrote:

He has said to me, "My grace is sufficient for you, for power is perfected in weakness." Most gladly, therefore, I will rather boast about my weaknesses, so that the power of Christ may dwell in me. Therefore I delight in weaknesses, in insults, in distresses, in persecutions, in difficulties, in behalf of Christ; for when I am weak, then I am strong.
(2 CORINTHIANS 12:9-10)

What does this tell us about God's grace? We need it every day of our lives. But we don't deserve it — it comes in God's packages according to His timing, according to His measure. We should receive each of those packages with massive amounts of thanksgiving!

GRACE TO CHANGE

When I was in my early twenties, I got a lot of grace, but I was too naive to know I was getting it. I got away with a lot of things, but I didn't change. I did my own thing. I took the grace for granted.

God gives us grace which puts up a red flag that says, "You need to change!" But we ignore them — never opening that gift, never using it; then finally God says, "Okay then. I'm going to make you change publicly." I propose to you that even some well-known ministers have had scandals in their ministries, but those scandals didn't pop up overnight. They knew about these things for a long time.

From God's view, the whole point of this isn't to expose and embarrass us; His purpose is eternal. So, a little public exposure might just change our heart, and that's what God is after — a change. Not just the little things or the embarrassment. He's interested in our eternity. He gives us grace so that we can change. Look at Romans 5:20–21:

> *The Law came in so that the offense would increase; but where sin increased, grace abounded all the more, so that, as sin reigned in death, so also grace would reign through righteousness to eternal life through Jesus Christ our Lord.*

Have you ever noticed that it seems the people who are getting a lot of grace — sinners — get away with their sin again and again? But the whole time, God is saying, "Grace! Grace! It's not for you to abuse; it's for you to change!"

Have you ever thought, *Why do they get away with that?* They don't; it's a grace opportunity. They're not getting away with it. God is trying to get their attention.

He says, "Look, you need to change. You didn't get in trouble this time, but this is your opportunity — by My goodness — to help you change!" It's with His goodness that He's trying to affect the change in us. What is He looking for? A change in the heart which yields righteous behavior (Romans 5:21).

Now, let's look at 2 Corinthians 6:1, *"And working together with Him, we also urge you not to receive the grace of God in vain."* Do we get God's grace but receive it in vain? "What a lovely gift! I'm glad I didn't get fired at my job." Then we just keep doing the same things over and over. That's not why we received grace! We receive grace in order to say, "Now that I see truth, I better adjust myself and make a change!"

PEOPLE GRACE

On the flip side of this, we're going to see that we get "people grace." Remember, we talked about what happens when someone likes you and you can't figure out why? That's an open door. That's God's gift of grace to witness.

We have people who help us with our makeup and hair for the television program, and they're always telling us, "I like to come here. This is a great place. I always leave here encouraged. I like you, Sarah." It's not that they don't like me; but they mostly like Jesus in me! It's grace. Grace is God at work.

Now, look at Ephesians Chapter 3:8: *"To me, the very least of all saints, this grace was given, to preach to the Gentiles the unfathomable riches of Christ."* Grace was given to Paul — not just to change his behavior — but so that he would go out and win people. We all have friends; they are opportunities, open doors.

Grace has been described as "God's unmerited favor." I don't know about you, but that sounds kind of religious to me. What does that mean, "unmerited favor"? It's something I didn't earn. What it means is: when we get down to where the rubber meets the road, grace is an opportunity given by God, along with His power to change.

GRACE-LACED WORDS

The next Scripture is also important: *"Let no unwholesome word come out of your mouth, but if there is any good word for edification according to the need of the moment, say that, so that it will give grace to those who hear"* (Ephesians 4:29).

We are supposed to speak in such a way that it gives grace to the hearers. We need to be full of grace so that our words are laced with grace. The way we stay full of grace is by receiving it and giving it out again. You want grace? Then give it. It's the same principle as sowing and reaping. You want people to have grace and mercy on you? Then you give it and you'll receive it.

ATTITUDE GRACE

Now let's see a little more about "attitude grace." How does attitude grace work with offerings?

"For you know the grace of our Lord Jesus Christ, that though He was rich, yet for your sake He became poor, so that you through His poverty might become rich" (2 Corinthians 8:9). Sometimes we are just flat-out stingy. We look in our wallets.

We've got a five, a one, and a ten, and we know — because we always keep a little hidden place — we've got a twenty in there. Or worse: when we look in the wallet and there's nothing there, but in the back of our minds we know we've got that spare twenty hidden in that little secret part — and it's offering time! What are we going to do?

"Well, I've got to save that emergency money. I can't give that." We get stingy. When we receive the offering at church, you can see it on people's faces as they're going through their wallets. You can see the struggle between greed and grace!

When will we ever get out of the poverty mentality and switch that for generosity with God? When we get attitude grace, then offering time is an opportunity for us to change and to say, "Truly, God is first in my finances."

THE DESTINY OF GRACE

There is a great passage of destiny found in Galatians:

> *But when He who had set me apart even from my mother's womb and called me through His grace was pleased to reveal His Son in me so that I might preach Him among the Gentiles, I did not immediately consult with flesh and blood.*
> **(GALATIANS 1:15-16)**

From his mother's womb, Paul had a destiny, and it was grace working on him and in him that revealed his destiny to him. We have a destiny; we have a goal.

Have you ever played darts? You don't aim for the outside — you aim for the bull's eye, the center. That's the destiny God has for you. Each experience we have with grace is a chance to hit the mark, to say,

"Yeah, that's my destiny. I nailed that one smack in the middle. That's a bullseye!" God has a destiny for each of us. We fulfill it by His grace, and His grace to change us.

OUR TALENTS AND GRACE

First Peter says, *"As each one has received a special gift, employ it in serving one another as good stewards of the multifaceted grace of God"* (1 Peter 4:10).

Whatever our talents and gifts, they're not just for our own benefit — they are to benefit each other. We see this time and time again at church and work. Some of the people I work with amaze me because their gifts are so wonderful. I think, *Wow, I'm so glad that person has that gift, because if I were trying to do it, it would be a waste!* I am personally blessed by their gifts.

As members of the body of Christ, we must not think, *I have to be called into full-time ministry to do that.* Not at all. In fact, any kind of opportunity we have to serve, to volunteer, is an opportunity for grace to change us.

Grace takes our talents and redirects them toward God's purpose. Look at Paul's pre-grace state: he was violent, zealous, aggressive, restless, cruel, and vindictive. These are all "natural attributes" — or talents, gifts — that Paul had, and they were well documented. So how did God use them?

Let's examine them. Zealous for God — could that be used in a positive way? Yes! After God touched him, that zealousness turned into a benefit. He wrote 13 books of the Bible. That's a huge benefit of grace.

How about violent? I would not consider violence to be a talent. So that's obviously a write-off, a bad characteristic. But how about aggressive? Saul was aggressive "before grace" and then, "after grace," God took that talent and used it for

His purposes. Paul was constantly moving, going after it. That ties in perfectly with being restless. He was restless before grace, but when grace touched him, God used his restlessness to put the church on the map. Look at all the churches he was instrumental in either founding or helping. He was, in a lot of respects, a father of the church.

God will take our talents in His hand and redirect them for His purposes, and not just for our benefit. Remember the widow in 1 Kings 17? She had a little bit of meal and a little bit of oil in her hands. But when we put our talents into God's hands — it never runs out, but it grows and grows, and we'll be doing what we never thought we possibly could do.

I see that with myself. I thought I would never, ever get to preach the Word in some of the places I've been, and I'm thrilled by it! It also motivates me because I have a vision and a passion to preach the Word in places that aren't open right now. I am determined to preach in China!

You watch! God is going to take my talent and, by His grace, He is going to open the door and put that talent to use. I just know that God will make it happen! I'm going to teach in places like China, where — right now — the doors are closed. When we put our talent in God's hands, He'll take us further than we ever thought we'd go in our own natural ability. That's God's plan.

What are your strengths that God may be redirecting? What are your talents? What are the things you do well? Is God saying, "I want you to change this a little bit"?

WINNING THROUGH GRACE

We've learned about grace touching us and changing us, our attitudes, and our hearts. We get the gift of grace for a change and also for victory. The best way to win is through grace. Romans 5:17 says, *"For if by the offense of the one, death reigned through the one, much more will those who receive the abundance of grace and of the gift of righteousness reign in life through the One, Jesus Christ."*

This means you and me — we who receive an abundance of grace and the gift of righteousness — will reign in life, and it starts with grace to change. Truly, we can be kings and queens in this life. But, in order to live the victorious life through grace, we must understand these three points:

#1: Repent for getting grace and not using it for its purpose. We've all received grace — and I hate to say this, but it's the truth — we've received grace in vain. Some of us have abused grace.

We've had good things happen, various opportunities where we were given nice things, or somebody was gracious to us, and we've said, "Whatever," and went on doing the same thing. We have all abused and misused grace, and we need to say, "God, where have I missed your grace? I was ungrateful for the grace that I got on the traffic ticket. Father, I'm sorry. Forgive me. Thank you for that opportunity to change." As we repent, we become grateful for those opportunities, grateful for that grace.

#2: Ask God for seeing eyes and hearing ears for the grace factor in our lives. When we receive grace, we don't shrug it off, saying, "Wow! I got away with that. Thanks!" No, we ask God to give us hearing ears and seeing eyes, so that we know: "That's grace!"

#3: Use grace as a catalyst for change in our lives. Grace is an opportunity to use the power of God to change. Saul received a grace package on the Damascus Road, and it changed him.

How about us? Maybe we don't have a big turning point, a huge Damascus Road experience, but what about the little ones we get? What are we going to do with it? We've got to determine that *"His grace toward me did not prove vain."* How about you? Will grace to you be in vain? Grace is for change. May we not get the grace in vain. May we not abuse grace, and may we not misuse grace. May God give us the grace to change so that when we see those opportunities, our eyes are open and our ears alert.

Chapter Three

GRACE TO REACH THE LOST

To start this third part, I strongly recommend you take the time to read all four chapters of the book of Jonah. You'll find it's about one of the worst complainers in the entire Bible. Right now, we're going to focus on Jonah 1 and 2.

WORTHLESS IDOLS

To understand more about God's dynamite packages of grace that He gives to us regularly, perhaps we should start by looking at the things we cling to that could cause us to miss out on receiving our grace packages from God. Here's a paraphrased quotation from Jonah 2:8 that helps start us off: "Those who cling to worthless idols forfeit the grace that could be theirs."

We all have different "idols" in our lives. We hold on to silly things. "Oh, I've got to do it my way. Oh, I've got to have this thing." I would propose this: maybe we ourselves are the biggest idols. "I live for me, and that's it." We cling to worthless idols.

Recently, I was telling a friend about something I was really struggling with, wondering whether or not to go and do something. She advised, "Sarah, it's all about you. You need to do what you want to do, and that's the bottom line."

That really caught me up short. I thought, *No, it's not all about me.* And I told my friend, "It's not all about me. It's about other people." If I cling to worthless idols, I'll neglect the true gift of grace. It's grace that will really change me.

Put yourself in Jonah's shoes for a moment. Here was a man who knew God, knew how to recognize the presence of God. Yet, when God sent him a task to do, he got stubborn and rebellious, and decided to try to run away from God. Three times in Jonah chapter one, it says that he tried to run away from the presence of God.

Jonah did his escaping-from-God thing, bought passage on a boat which was headed in the totally opposite direction from Nineveh, and he crept down into the very bottom of the boat and went to sleep. He probably reasoned to himself: *Maybe in my sleep, I won't hear the voice of God telling me to go to Nineveh.* For someone to sleep that soundly — especially once the storm started — I would suspect that Jonah probably had to "medicate" himself. That is, he probably drank himself into a sleeping, drunken stupor.

We try all sorts of ways to avoid God. Some people get really busy: "I'm just so busy with my work, my family, and with my self-improvement program. Maybe later I'll do something for you, God." Some people get really belligerent: "Aren't you supposed to be the God of everything? Then go find someone else to do your hard work. You can't possibly need me."

Some people hide behind their personal excuses: "Well, I'm certainly not educated enough to do something special for God" or "I don't have a 'call' on my life to be a minister. I'm just a regular churchgoer, and that's it."

Some people try the "avoidance behavior" route — which usually involves alcohol, drugs, or "enlightening experiences" — all sorts of ways to try stuffing something else into that "God-shaped place in the heart." It just doesn't work.

KNOWING THE PRESENCE OF GOD

Let's get back to Jonah. Once the storm started, the sailors all grew increasingly afraid. Finally:

Each man said to his mate, "Come, let's cast lots so that we may find out on whose account this catastrophe has struck us." So they cast lots, and the lot fell on Jonah. Then they said to him, "Tell us, now! On whose account has this catastrophe struck us? What is your occupation, and where do you come from? What is your country, and from what people are you?" **(JONAH 1:7-8)**

Jonah finally confessed to the sailors on the boat that the reason they were all about to die in the storm was because he was running away from God. He said, *"Pick me up and hurl me into the sea. Then the sea will become calm for you, because I know that on account of me this great storm has come upon you"* (Jonah 1:12).

Despite this difficult admission, the men on the boat were still willing to give him the benefit of the doubt, and they kept on trying to save the boat: *"However, the men rowed desperately to return to land, but they could not, because the sea was becoming even stormier against them"* (Jonah 1:13).

Finally, feeling very badly about it, they threw Jonah overboard.

In Jonah 2:1–9, the Bible records Jonah's prayer while he was in the belly of the whale. He finished the prayer with, *"Salvation is from the LORD"* (v. 9). He acknowledged that, even in the stomach of the fish, God was there. Talk about a strange place for Him to deliver a gift of grace! Jonah could not escape the presence of God, and so he repented. Then God spoke to the fish and it vomited Jonah onto dry land.

WHALE BELLY GRACE

The whale was uncomfortable. (Whether it was really a whale, we don't know. The Bible just calls it a great fish, but I like to think it was a whale, so that's what I'm going to call it.) The whale didn't like its "dinner," Jonah. It developed a huge belly ache and vomited Jonah out.

How many of us would willingly, eagerly, volunteer to spend three nights in a whale's belly? "All expenses paid! One-way ticket! Free swimming pool!" We'd all be signing up, right? I don't think so. A whale's belly is yucky, with all those smelly digestive juices. What if you spent three days in that mess? That's completely disgusting!

There are times when we get "whale belly grace." Events in our lives that have been really uncomfortable but that were instrumental in shaping and developing us. Just as Jonah was uncomfortable in the whale's belly (and the whale was uncomfortable with Jonah in its belly!), many of us have had uncomfortable situations. In essence, although it was uncomfortable, Jonah received "whale belly grace."

I know a Christian family whose teenaged daughter got pregnant and had a baby while unmarried. The whole family was ashamed and torn up about what seemed to be such a tragic thing — a teenage mother trying to raise a baby alone.

Years later, when the girl grew up and got married, she developed cancer. After all the radiation treatments and procedures, she was healed of the cancer. However, the young woman and her husband wanted to have more children, but the chemotherapy had made her infertile.

They all looked back at that time in her life when they thought the world was going to end — when she had a baby out of wedlock. And they thanked God that, although the whole family had been so uncomfortable when she got pregnant, at least they had a beautiful child and grandchild to love. We don't like it when we are uncomfortable, but we get "whale belly grace" nonetheless.

WHALE GRACE PACKAGES

We had a huge "whale belly grace" package with the terrible shooting at Columbine High School in the spring of 1999. Certainly, the murder and bloodshed were not from God, but look at the after-effects of what God did with the opportunities we had.

After the shootings, the school and government held a huge public memorial rally with people like Franklin Graham, Michael W. Smith, Phil Driscoll, and Amy Grant — all who unabashedly preached the gospel. I would call that "whale belly grace." How many people came to that rally? Over 18,000. And it was on CNN, with a television audience of probably millions. Wow — that was grace! We didn't like what happened, and it was tragic, but God used it.

Jonah probably hated the whale, but he liked the whale better than the alternative: drowning and death. He would rather stink and be uncomfortable for three days than die. Given that choice, I'd take the stink and being uncomfortable for three days!

God gives us grace that we have to use. We have no choice. I'll give you an example.

LEWIS AND LIBBY

When I was in my early twenties and a student at Oral Roberts University in Tulsa, Oklahoma, I was having a hard time with God. I basically came to the point where I was struggling in my heart. I was lonely, depressed, reaching out, and feeling there was no God. It was probably one of the darkest times of my life. I was searching, and here's what God brought to me.

First, I read *Mere Christianity* by C.S. Lewis. To me, that was "whale belly grace." God knew I had to have something. I read that book, and I said, "God, if you can take this little bit of faith..." (because at that point, I didn't believe in Jesus), "...it's yours. I have limited belief in you, but I have to have something!" That was "whale belly grace" to me.

Then He gave me another gift of "whale belly grace." This is so funny because "whale belly grace" comes in ways that we don't always like. All the students at ORU had to do a jogging test at the end of every semester. It was three miles, and I hated it with a passion. By my senior year — the first time I practiced for it — I said, "Okay, I'm going to try and run this thing to the best of my ability, but I need some help."

Interestingly enough, I was still struggling with God, still questioning, still searching, lonely, depressed, and having a hard time. But I was a "Resident Advisor," and one of my fellow R.A.'s was named Libby. Eventually, I learned to like Libby, but initially, I didn't like her because I didn't realize she was a gift of grace to me.

I was very athletic, while Libby was ultra-feminine. She was definitely not my style, and I wasn't her style, but somehow, we would get together a couple of times a week and jog.

During those jogs, she became a friend to me, and I could talk to her. I would talk to her about my struggles with God, and she would encourage me. She would be warm to me, not cold and heartless. She never said, "You're going to burn in hell for saying that!" She was a "whale belly grace" package.

I might not have initially liked how she looked, but she was a gift of grace. And the grace that she gave me helped me change. Libby was awesome.

Can we think of some of the different whale grace circumstances we've experienced in our lives? Maybe we didn't like them, but we certainly appreciated what He did for us! That is "whale belly grace."

Right now, you may be in the middle of a "whale belly grace" situation. Don't miss it. Don't say, "No thanks." That would be an awfully big gift to miss.

JONAH, CONTINUED

The next part is about Jonah's third gift of grace. Jonah was in the whale for three days, and finally, the whale got sick and vomited Jonah up on the beach. Personally, considering how obnoxious Jonah was — especially in his conversations with God — I think the whale had a right to dislike the taste of Jonah!

Anyway, here came Jonah flopping out, and he was all covered with vomit. That was the condition in which he was going to go preach to Nineveh. "Here I come!" He looked awful, he smelled awful, he had a lousy attitude, and he said, "Look out, Nineveh, here I come, and I've got a terribly hard message for you. You are all going to die!"

If you were one of the inhabitants of Nineveh and here came this vomit-covered man out of the ocean yelling at you, "In 40 days, God is going to destroy you!" What would you think? God's next grace package for Jonah was that the people didn't blow him off! They didn't lock him up. They didn't say he was a lunatic and probably dangerous.

They didn't say, "Watch out for that guy. He's all covered with whale slime and vomit. He's probably contagious as well as crazy." Instead, the people did none of that. They listened to him and repented.

God was so gracious to him that even the king said, "Okay, let's repent." The king put everybody on a holy fast, even the animals. The Ninevites were not church people. They didn't really know what to do, but they knew they had to honor God and the man of God.

Think about the people in your neighborhood. Think of the people about whom we've possibly said in the past, "They'll never, never, never come to Christ." Or maybe we've said, "They seem like the hardest people ever. God, just forget them."

Look at the grace God gave to Jonah. He preached in a huge city. The Bible says it took three days to walk across Nineveh. Jonah walked in, and he didn't even try that hard. He smelled like vomit; he looked like vomit. He had just been in a whale's belly for three days.

He walked into this big city and was there for three days, right in front of them. *"Jonah began to go through the city one day's walk; and he cried out and said, 'Forty more days, and Nineveh will be overthrown'"* (Jonah 3:4).

That's all he said. He didn't say, "Repent!" He didn't say, "God loves you. He is gracious. He is merciful." He said none of that, but look at the people's responsiveness!

> *Then the people of Nineveh believed in God; and they called a fast and put on sackcloth, from the greatest to the least of them. When the word reached the king of Nineveh, he got up from his throne, removed his robe from himself, covered himself with sackcloth, and sat on the dust. And he issued a proclamation, and*

it said, "In Nineveh by the decree of the king and his nobles: No person, animal, herd, or flock is to taste anything. They are not to eat, or drink water. But every person and animal must be covered with sackcloth; and people are to call on God vehemently, and they are to turn, each one from his evil way, and from the violence which is in their hands. Who knows, God may turn and relent, and turn from His burning anger so that we will not perish." **(JONAH 3:5-9)**

These were people who had never had an encounter with God, who didn't know anything about Jehovah, but they repented!

Now, do you think God could use you the same way? Could He use you to reach the unsaved? When souls are at stake, it costs too much to reject God's grace.

GRACE RESPONSES

Now, let's look at some modern examples of God's grace packages. One time, I had a neighbor who said to me, "You know, my house is a mess. I hate my house. We just built it, but it's a mess. I hate it. Everything's wrong about it" — and I just knew it was an opportunity for grace.

Do you ever get tired of people complaining? Instead of seeing it as a complaint, we should look at it as an opportunity. What they're really saying is, "Something is wrong in my life."

This neighbor kept complaining, and I said, "You know, that's too bad, but you can have all that going on on the outside and still have peace in your heart, and that peace comes from Jesus." Another friend once asked, "What do you think about the year 2000 thing — you know, 'Y2K' and all these problems? Don't you think we ought to be hiding food, stocking up, and being crazy like everybody else?" (This was a person who didn't go to church.)

I said, "No, I don't think so. I think we're putting the cart before the horse. We're concerned about our physical bodies, and we're neglecting our eternity." It was an opportunity. When somebody's complaining — see it as an opportunity! People say they have needs. We have the answer!

SALT AND LIGHT

Recently, I was watching a television show where they were talking about people who commit rape multiple times. The courts were considering castration as a means of punishment for these criminals. *Castration?* I thought. *That's terrible. Castration isn't going to change the heart.*

I thank God I am in the profession that changes hearts. And you are too. Social problems aren't solved on the surface — they're solved in the heart. And we've got the answer! We are the salt. We are the light.

> *"You are the salt of the earth; but if the salt has become tasteless, how can it be made salty again? It is no longer good for anything, except to be thrown out and trampled underfoot by people. You are the light of the world. A city set on a hill cannot be hidden; nor do people light a lamp and put it under a basket, but on the lampstand, and it gives light to all who are in the house. Your light must shine before people in such a way that they may see your good works, and glorify your Father who is in heaven."*
> **(MATTHEW 5:13-16)**

Jonah said, "Okay, I'll go, and I'll preach." And he barely said anything when God blew the doors wide open. How about with us? "Well, what if I don't do it right?" It won't be the first time we don't do it right, and it won't be the last time, but it doesn't mean we quit trying.

Jonah was extremely happy to get "whale belly grace." He got saved from drowning. "Thank you, God, for the whale belly grace." But are we just as quick to give it out? When someone is being mean, crude, and rude, we like to get the grace, but are we quick to give it out?

Let's not hold back on grace. What you sow is what you reap. If you want grace, sow grace. If you want forgiveness, sow it. These are important keys when we handle grace, so we don't abuse it and mishandle it.

VINE GRACE

Now, finally, the fourth kind of grace is "vine grace." It seems from the account in

Jonah 3 that he preached kind of half-heartedly, "Hey, in 40 days, y'all are going to die. See you!" and he left. Then in chapter 4, it says that he climbed a hill, sat down, and watched the city to see what was going to happen. He was hoping that the city would be destroyed, but it wasn't. Jonah then said, "God, I'm mad at you."

God said, "Why are you mad at me?"

Jonah answered, "Because you are loving, gracious, kind, and forgiving, and I knew you were going to save that city, and I didn't want you to." That's exactly what he said.

Sometimes we're that way. We get mad at God. "I don't like that you've been good to them. They didn't deserve it." Does that sound familiar?

God said to Jonah, "Do you have any right to be mad at me?"

"Yes, I have a right." That's so lame! It was like Jonah pouted and said, "Fine!" and then pouted some more. Here's what happened next...

He was sitting up on this hill in the heat, watching the city, and he built a shelter for himself. He was getting an attitude. He was upset and thought, *This is the pits. God is going to save them, and they should have burned in hell.* But the neat thing is: even when he was showing all of his attitude and garbage, God still sent him grace in the form of a vine.

Jonah was parked up on the hill, having a good pout, and here came the vine. The Bible said it offered him shade and comfort, and he liked it.

By day two, he found there was a worm that had eaten the vine a little bit. It started to wither, so he perched himself under the half-withered vine. Soon the sun came out, with scorching heat and bad wind, and he was hot.

If we thought he had a bad attitude before, now he really flew off the handle! He raged, "Oh, this is so bad! I should have died. I just want to die! This is so horrible! They're being saved. I'm uncomfortable. I want to die right now!"

Then God asked him, "Is it right for you to be angry about the plant? Are you sure you're supposed to be angry?"

Jonah replied, "Yeah, it's right. It's right, even to the point of death. Kill me. I'm so mad about this plant." To which God said:

> *You had compassion on the plant, for which you did not work and which you did not cause to grow, which came up overnight and perished overnight. Should I not also have compassion on Nineveh, the great city in which there are more than 120,000 people, who do not know*

the difference between their right hand and their left, as well as many animals? **(JONAH 4:10-11)**

When we receive the grace factor, we walk on the enemy, because God's grace is given to us simply because He loves us — not because we deserve it — it's His loving provision.

REACHING PEOPLE

We previously discussed the definition of grace as "God's unmerited favor." I want to remind you that grace is really a God-given opportunity, with His power, to change and reach people! We must have God's grace to reach people.

When the Columbine High School massacre happened, a lot of Christians said, "Oh, we've got to reach people. We've got to get souls!" — as if suddenly it had become really important. But I would say to you it was just as important before the Columbine massacre. Do we have to have a massacre to motivate us? God forgive us if that's the truth.

A man in Castle Rock, Colorado, drove up to the police station and shot at the police through the window of his car. The police came running out and said to him, "Drop the gun!" But he didn't do it. For whatever reason, he provoked the police. Then the police shot him and killed him. They didn't know what was going on with him. They searched his car and discovered that he had shot his three little girls, all of them under ten years old.

We need to reach people. We have always needed to reach people.

In 1993, Steven Spielberg put out a movie called *Schindler's List* about the Holocaust during World War II, when the Jews were being forced into slave labor for the Nazis before they killed them. There was a Czech

Nazi industrialist, Oskar Schindler, who, at first, cooperated with the Nazis, using the imprisoned Jews as his unpaid labor force.

As time went on, Schindler's heart began to soften toward the Jews, so he turned all his energy, all his fortune, to helping the Jews escape the concentration camps and extermination camps. Toward the end of the movie, there is a scene which is heart-stopping. The war has just ended, and now Schindler knows he will be liable for trial as a Nazi sympathizer. Although he had spent his fortune saving Jewish lives, now he was the criminal.

However, the Jews didn't view him that way; they came to say goodbye to Oskar Schindler and to honor him for all he had done for them. Schindler was deeply moved. He had done a lot of things to save the Jews from concentration camps, spending all his money to save their lives. Yet when he saw his expensive car, he practically fell down in front of it, saying, "This car could have saved ten people!" He was sobbing. Then he fumbled around and saw a pin on his jacket. "This is a solid gold pin. I could have gotten out at least one person with this pin. I didn't do enough! I didn't do enough!"

Have we done enough?

THE GOAL OF GRACE

We tend to set limits on what we do and don't do. We say, "It's enough if I do this, and then I don't have to do any more than that. It's enough if I witness to my neighbor once, and then I don't have to do any more than that."

In God's economy, He said it was enough when He sent Jesus to die. But have we gone to that limit? Have we become a living sacrifice to reach people? How does this relate to grace? Not only is the grace intended to help us change, but it's also to reach people.

We have to get to people. In most churches, we have special speakers and evangelists specifically gifted to bring in the lost, but we can't just rely on Sunday mornings and special speakers to reach the lost. There are people killing their kids because they have no God. There are children shooting other children because they have no God. We don't just get grace for us to change and be better; we get grace to reach people.

The goal of grace has two parts — essentially, two sides of the same coin. One side is to help change us, and the other side is to reach people.

Jonah had four different kinds of grace that he received: a storm, a whale, people's responsiveness, and a vine for shade. Let's look again at God's assignment to Jonah. God spoke to Jonah very decisively, very authoritatively, and told him, "That is your assignment, bud. I need you to go do this," and He gave him very direct, explicit instructions. Jonah 1:1–2 says: *"The word of the Lord came to Jonah the son of Amittai, saying, 'Arise, go to Nineveh, the great city, and cry out against it, because their wickedness has come up before Me.'"*

That was Jonah's assignment. The instructions in this grace to Jonah were his opportunity. "I need you to go do this." It was God's power. What He tells us to do, He is going to enable us to do.

This grace was also for Jonah to change, so he would reach out to the people of Nineveh so that they would come to know God and have an opportunity to receive grace. But this was what Jonah said: "Okay. I get the grace. I totally understand what you're trying to tell me to do, but I'm not interested. No way."

When we reject grace, life goes downhill. We think we can reject grace and limit our plunge — limit how far down we will go. Jonah reasoned, *I can go down into the ship, take a nap, and go to sleep.* But that wasn't the furthest down he went! Because in chapter 2, we learned that he goes much, much farther down!

He went down into the depths of the ocean! If we reject grace, our decline is not going to be limited to ourselves. It's going to be beyond what we can control. We cannot afford to reject grace — it will cost us even more than we can calculate.

Jonah paid the fare and stepped on the ship headed for Tarshish and away from Nineveh — away from the presence of the Lord. Not only was he saying, "No thanks," but he was saying, "I'm out of here. I want to get far away from God." So, he ran.

Jonah's goals conflicted with God's goals. God's goals were for Nineveh and to change Jonah's heart. Jonah was saying, "I'm not doing that. I have my own goals. I'm going to do my own thing." How many times do we say that?

We hear God's goals: "Win the lost, make disciples, reach the nations." We get pumped up in a church service, but when we leave, our attitude reverts to, "See you! I got to do my own thing." We cannot afford to do that; it costs too much, and the world is going to hell too fast for us to be self-centered!

The old saying is all too true: your feet will take you where your heart already is. The fact that you're reading this book tells you something about where your heart is. You could be anywhere, doing anything, but your feet have taken you to a place where your heart says, "I want to hear from God!" That's awesome!

STORM GRACE

Like Jonah, we can be in denial of our problems and miss out on God's grace. While sleeping at the very bottom of the boat, Jonah received another package of grace. He got "storm grace." A storm broke out, the boat was rocking back and forth, pitching, having a hard time. The wind was blowing. It was so bad that even the sailors were freaked out about it. They were so uptight they were throwing their profit — the cargo — into the water. They were bowing down to their gods, crying, "God (whoever you are), help us, help us!" And there was Jonah, snoring!

Now notice this: Jonah was in this boat; the storm came; it was an opportunity for Jonah to change and reach the people, but he was sleeping. He was totally blowing it off. The sailors' lives were at risk because of Jonah's disobedience. Those sailors wouldn't be bailing water, praying to their gods, crying, "Help us!" and throwing cargo over if Jonah wasn't in their boat, disobeying God, saying, "No thanks."

We don't evaluate how severe it is until we start to count the cost in people's lives. We have to count the cost — not just in money, not just in time, not just with our energy. We have to count the cost in lives, in people, because that's the true estimation. That's how God measures it and sees it: people, souls, and eternity.

Sometimes we exchange our souls for less than what they're really worth. The cost of our souls was the life of Jesus Christ. Yet we're selling them for entertainment, for money, for whatever. Some of us are a real bargain for the devil. "Entertain her. You can get her for just a movie." We sell our souls for less than what God paid for them.

The captain came down and woke up Jonah. "Wake up, you fool! Don't you know we're going to perish? Pray to your God so that we won't perish!" What did Jonah do? Zip. He didn't do anything. He didn't pray. He was selfish. The lives of the captain and the sailors were at risk, and he knew it was all because of his disobedience. He thought, *Okay, they'll drown with me. Who cares?* Wow.

God, give us grace that we are not so callous with people in our neighborhood or with people at our work!

We must never think, *Oh well, it's just another person, another soul, another eternity.* That's not the same value that Christ sees in us or in the souls around us.

The sailors were so uptight, they demanded to find out who had caused the storm. They drew straws and said, "Uh oh, it's Jonah. What's the problem, Jonah?"

Then Jonah admitted, "Look, if you throw me over, everything will be fine." This was really a man with a death wish! He told the sailors, "I'm running to get away from God. I'm just trying to get away from Him."

When the sailors heard this, they said, "You want us to kill you, to throw you overboard, so that we can save ourselves? We're not going to do that." So they rowed all the harder. The more they did, the worse the storm got.

Once they threw him over, the sea got calm. Do you realize that Jonah was the obstacle to the sailors' salvation? The Bible says, *"Then the men became extremely afraid of the Lord, and they offered a sacrifice to the Lord and made vows"* (Jonah 1:16). They stopped praying to their alternate false gods, and they prayed to the Lord. Is it possible that we can be obstacles to someone's salvation?

OBSTACLES

Are we barriers or conduits for God's grace? We get His grace; we like it; it helps us; it changes us; but are we conduits of God's grace for the people around us? Does grace flow through us to grab them and save them from hell?

When a friend of mine was traveling with a group of young Christians, they went to Amsterdam's red-light district. This is probably one of the raunchiest places on the planet, absolutely godless in some respects. But she went and saw everything that was going on. She was young — in her early twenties. It shook her to the core.

She left and went back to the place where some of her Christian friends were gathered. They were making jokes about the stuff that was going on in the red-light district. They were making jokes about the people, about the tragedy of what was going on there, and laughing about it. "Come on!" she protested. "Those are souls!"

May we not be a barrier or obstacle between God and people! "God, I want to be very efficient in your hands so that when I die, you will say, 'Well done.'"

Jonah was a very stubborn man. He valued doing his own thing more than he valued obeying God. He received God's assignment and said, "No thanks, I'm not interested."

His disobedience and stubbornness put a lot of people in jeopardy — the sailors, the people of Nineveh, and himself. Our attitude in life should never be, "I'm just going to sit here being a Christian, knowing that I've got my heavenly insurance policy, and if I don't bother anybody else, then everything will be alright." No! God gives us His grace to change us and to affect the lives of other people!

"Go into all the world and preach the gospel to all creation" (Mark 16:15). This is God's assignment, a command to every

believer, not just to preachers and pastors. If we say "no thanks," we are condemning the world to hell. Our inactivity puts people's lives in danger. We can't just stay isolated and safe! We must receive grace and accept our responsibility to be salt and light to the world.

SOLUTIONS

> *"What person is there among you who, when his son asks for a loaf of bread, will give him a stone? Or if he asks for a fish, he will not give him a snake, will he? So if you, despite being evil, know how to give good gifts to your children, how much more will your Father who is in heaven give good things to those who ask Him!"* **(MATTHEW 7:9-11)**

Have you got it? Do you understand? God's solution for your every situation is called "grace." Do you have tangled relationships or financial predicaments? Do you want to be happy and successful? Then don't miss the grace factor — even if it comes in an unusual circumstance or isn't what you want, expect, or hope for from God. Please don't say, "No thanks." God's grace is your ultimate solution — so grab the grace, whether it's the grace to get you through, the grace to change, or the grace that enables you to reach out to others.

You've got real problems, and God has the genuine answers. He isn't mad at you. He loves you more than you can imagine. Trust Him as you would a devoted father! God isn't going to hand you a snake when you need a means of escape or toss you a stone instead of a solution.

THE GRACE FACTOR

Grace is given to us for three reasons: to get us through, to change us, and to enable us to reach out to others and be a conduit of God's grace to the world. We've learned a lot about grace, but you may never have personally experienced God's grace through His Son Jesus. If you've never asked Jesus into your heart, that's the first step to receiving grace from the creator of this universe. You say, "I want to receive grace. I want to receive Jesus into my heart. I want that relationship with Jesus. I need grace."

Maybe you've backslidden or denied Him. I want to give you the opportunity right now to accept the author of grace. He has been so good to you, but maybe you've pushed Him away for whatever reason. You need to make a fresh commitment to Jesus. Boldly say, "Yes, I need a fresh touch of grace. I need a fresh commitment with

Jesus." If that's you, then do it now. You know He's good. You know He loves you. You know He's after your heart.

This is God's grace tugging at your heart. He's calling, "Come to Me. It's not just that you get your sins forgiven, it's that you will walk with Me." That's His grace pulling on you. Don't reject it. Don't let His grace be without effect in your life.

Say "Yes" to God's grace.

RECEIVE JESUS CHRIST AS LORD AND SAVIOR OF YOUR LIFE

You can have Jesus's joy, peace, protection, and provision in your life starting today. You can also know for sure that you will have life after death in heaven.

God sent Jesus Christ to be the Savior of the world. First Timothy 2:5–6 says, *"For there is one God and one Mediator between God and men, the Man Christ Jesus, who gave Himself a ransom for all, to be testified in due time."*

The Bible tells us how we can receive Jesus as Savior:

If you confess with your mouth the Lord Jesus and believe in your heart that God has raised Him from the dead, you will be saved. For with the heart one believes unto righteousness, and with the mouth confession is made unto salvation.
(ROMANS 10:9-10)

Would you like to begin a personal relationship with God and Jesus right now? You can! Simply pray this prayer in sincerity:

Heavenly Father, I acknowledge that I need your help. I am not able to change my life or circumstances through my own efforts. I know that I have made some wrong decisions in my life, and at this moment I turn away from those ways of thinking and acting. I believe you have provided a way for me through Jesus to receive your blessings and help in my life. Right now, I believe and confess Jesus as my Lord and Savior. I ask Jesus to come into my heart and give me a new life, by your Spirit. I thank you for saving me and I ask for your grace and mercy in my life. I pray this in Jesus's name. Amen.

If you just prayed to make Jesus your Lord, we want to know!

Please call us today — toll free — at 888-637-4545.

We will pray for you and send you a special gift to help you in your new life with Christ.

TO LEARN MORE ABOUT SARAH BOWLING, VISIT:

SARAH BOWLING — LIVING GENUINE LOVE: SARAHBOWLING.ORG

Check out Sarah's blog posts, podcasts, videos, and more!

ONLINE CLASSROOM: LEARNINGGENUINELOVE.ORG

Grab a cup of coffee and join Sarah for an adventure with Holy Spirit!

CONNECT WITH SARAH:

- SarahGenuineLove
- SarahBowling
- Sarah_GenuineLove
- SarahBowlingLivingGenuineLove